THE SECRETS TO SELLING
ON
AMAZON

HOW TO
MASTER THE SKILL
OF BUYING LOW
AND SELLING HIGH

BEAU CRABILL

The Secrets to Selling on Amazon

How I Turned Nothing into Million$

By Beau Crabill

ACKNOWLEDGMENTS

Along with all the practical reasons for writing this book, publishing it provides an opportunity to devote this body of work and say thank you—to three very special people.

The first of those three, is you.

Without you, it is likely that this book may never have been written. You gave me a purpose, and the desire, and the willingness to write it.

I feel that I am always in a constant battle online. There are haters, there are scammers, there are people who over-promise and under-deliver. There are opportunities that come and go. However, the one constant and continually inspiring aspect of this business for me, is the interaction I have with all the determined, enthusiastic and dedicated people who get involved in my program—because they are seeking a greater education in order to better themselves. I love getting encouraging messages on my Instagram, YouTube, and Facebook accounts, or receiving emails from people who want to share their success stories with me. It is great to find out how their business has changed, and how their mindset has shifted after encountering information they've found through my sites.

I am proud of the fact that, regardless of my young age, I have been able to establish myself as an outlet where students can find the best possible education and the most useful information resources available in the eCommerce space.

So, thank you. If it were not for you, this book would not have been possible.

Secondly, I want to thank my mentor, Steven Sitkowski.

The life that I am living today, the positive impact that I am able to have on my students and followers, and the people that will benefit from this program in the future—and even the overall positive mindset I have—none of these things would be possible without Steve and all that he has taught me and shared with me in recent years. I am a firm believer in the law of attraction. It is not that I believe that you merely think of something and then it just happens. I believe the process works more similarly to the way that magnets operate. There is personal action required. If you place two magnets too far away from each other, nothing happens. However, when two magnets are in proximity, a reaction occurs. By making the choice to closely align myself with Steven in Utah, great things have emerged from that connection. I am extremely proud of the person I am today, but I would not be where I am had it not been for my mentor Steve. Thank you, Steve—I love you.

Finally, I would like to thank my father.

Hindsight is 20/20, as the adage goes. When I look back at all that my father taught me, there are three things that seem most important:

- Have a strong work ethic.

- Have integrity.

- Learn from your own mistakes and from other people's mistakes as well.

I am the youngest of three siblings. Our family dynamic and our home environment were not always especially pleasant, to put it mildly. Sadly, the fact is that our mother was a severe alcoholic. My dad struggled financially from making numerous unprofitable mistakes. My siblings and I did not always get along when we were young. Overall, my childhood was far from idyllic. This sort of tumultuous upbringing can have any number of deleterious impacts on a child, but, in my case, my childhood experiences actually instilled in me the distinct understanding that I needed to grow up fast and that I needed to find a new and different way to live, rather than mimicking many of the examples I'd seen in my own family life. In a way, my experiences fueled my drive to educate myself and to become independent, as soon as possible.

Going back to some of my earliest clear memories, I was the kind of person that tended to plan ahead. I can recall that at just eight years of age, I was imagining what I wanted to be doing at age twenty, and thirty, and forty.

Throughout all his entrepreneurial ventures, my Dad tried to involve me in his business activities. He was selling on eBay, off and on. When I was nine years old, I would help him out with his online sales listings. While I was still in elementary school, I helped him out with a paper route in the very early hours of some cold Washington mornings.

My dad taught me the important principal of never giving up—to learn to persist when most everyone else was quitting. I believe that learning this principal at a young age helped give me the perseverance I needed to become a top athlete in endurance running. From Dad's teachings, I developed a tenacious determination which allows me to perform well when working the long hours that are often a necessary part of accomplishing the challenging and important goals I set for myself.

My dad would often talk about the importance of acting with integrity. He lived by the mantra: "Do the right thing, whether or not you think anyone is watching." From his example, I learned to live by this tenet also, and doing so has paid off in massive ways in my life. I am amazed— dismayed, actually—when I see just how many people try to take shortcuts to success in business. It seems that there are not many people that have been taught that taking the time to do things the right way—even if that means it takes a little longer to get things going at the start—will result in greater success in the long run.

Lastly, from my Dad I learned the value of learning from mistakes, both my own errors, and those made by other people. My dad knew that he was not perfect. He didn't try to pretend that he was exempt from making bad decisions. From the time I was very young, my dad wanted me to learn to be self-aware and to recognize when I needed to make corrections or adjustments with my own behavior, and he taught me the usefulness of learning from other people's mistakes as well

I may not have been fully aware of all these great lessons my father was instilling in me while they were happening, that is why I made my earlier comment about hindsight being 20/20. When I consider the early success I have had in business and all the success I am enjoying today, my instinct is to think that the way I approach things in life and the methods I use for making decisions, are just borne from common sense—and that sensibility feels like something that is just my nature. In reality, the reason much of it feels innate to me, is that it is the result of the remarkable parenting and nurturing I got from my Dad, since I was very young, and it is inextricably a part of who I am and how I see the world. Love you Dad.

DISCLAIMER

Any income or earnings statements are estimates of income potential only, and there is no assurance that your earnings will match the figures presented, which are given as examples.

Your reliance on the figures we present is at your own risk. Any income or earnings depicted are **not** to be interpreted as common, typical, expected, or normal for the average Student.

Particular results may be exceptional, and the variables that impact results are so numerous and sometimes uncontrollable, we make no guarantees as to your income or earnings of any kind, at any time. All testimonials are a result of personal experience or were provided by each individual. These testimonials have **not** been verified for accuracy or truthfulness; and although believed to be completely accurate, should not be used as an indication or prediction of your results. There is no assurance that your earnings or income will match those figures, or that you will make any money at all. If you rely upon our examples or figures, you do so at your own risk, and you accept all risk associated with your reliance.

Any and all claims or representations as to income earnings made on our websites or in our materials or information are not to be considered as average earnings. Testimonials are not representative. There can be no assurances that any prior successes, or past results, as to income results, can be used as an indication of your future success or results. Monetary and income results are based on many factors. Each individual's success depends on his or her background, work ethic, dedication, desire, and motivation; as well as other factors not always known and sometimes beyond your control.

Therefore, we do not guarantee or imply that you will make any income or earnings, or that you will make any money at all.

As with any business endeavor, there is an inherent risk of loss of capital and there is no guarantee that you will earn any money. Making decisions based on any information presented in our programs, products, services or on our website, should be done only with the knowledge that you could experience significant losses or make no money at all. Only risk capital should be used.

Contents

ACKNOWLEDGMENTS   v

DISCLAIMER   ix

INTRODUCTION   xi

PART ONE

INTRODUCTION

Chapter 1 Why You Should Sell on Amazon   2

Chapter 2 My Story   6

Chapter 3 Three Principles for Success with   29
           Selling on Amazon

PART TWO

START UP—STRATEGY—MY SYSTEM

Chapter 4 First Steps   40

Chapter 5 Product Analysis   50

Chapter 6 The Role of Suppliers   57

Chapter 7 Finding Suppliers   63

Chapter 8 Building Supplier Relationships   82

Chapter 9 Shipping to Amazon   86

Chapter 10 Getting Ungated   97

Chapter 11 Winning the Buy Box   102

Chapter 12 Simplify Your Process with Software   111

PART THREE

AMAZON LIFE THE PAST, PRESENT AND FUTURE

Chapter 13 Tough Lessons   124

Chapter 14 Success Stories   132

Chapter 15 The Future of My Amazon Business   155

Conclusion   160

INTRODUCTION

When I tell people that I'm 20 years old and I've sold over a million dollars online, the first question I'm asked usually involves an inquiry into which luxury cars I must own. So, I pull up my Amazon seller account and show them my Lamborghinis.

I bought 864 of them for $734.40.

1	CO-DWF21	12	CS	MATTEL HW LAMBORGHINI ASST	72	864	0.850	734.40

I'm talking about Hot Wheels Lamborghinis. Toys.

These Lambos were some of the most profitable products I've sold on Amazon. The toy car variety sold quickly—864 units (108 packs of eight toys) gone in two and a half weeks. With proof of demand I then ordered 8,000 additional units, at $6.80 per unit. As you can see here, each unit sold for $36.44.

Product Details	Unit price
Hot Wheels 2017 Lamborghini Bundle of 8 Die-Cast Vehicles 1:64 Scale	$36.44

 SKU: VO-G0WK-H8MN
ASIN: B074443YXN
⌄ Show more

After accounting for Amazon's fees for shipping and FBA (Fulfilment by Amazon—where Amazon handles the process of filling and shipping the order), you'll see that $19.50 was pure profit. That's almost a 300 percent ROI (return on investment). It is not that I expect that all my products will achieve such a high ROI, but I always calculate the return beforehand — and if the return is less than 10 percent, I won't invest. My average item achieves a 21.05 percent ROI.

More importantly, I only choose products that sell quickly. I'll happily sacrifice some ROI for a product that will make money fast, which allows me to make the most of the magic of compound interest. My goal is to generate a net profit of 10 percent per month across my product lines.

Amazon has experienced explosive growth over the past few years (with $232 billion in sales in 2018, and over 30 percent growth from 2017). With that growth, many self-described online sales gurus suddenly began to gravitate towards promoting courses for selling on Amazon. You may have seen these so-called experts' advertisements pop up on Facebook, Instagram, and YouTube, with many of them shouting about ARBITRAGE, DROPSHIPPING and PRIVATE LABELING—as they pose in front of their (probably rented) Lamborghinis.

So, what sets my advice apart from the advice of these supposed experts?

First, they are not knowledgeable. Many of these people who are promoting themselves as Amazon online sales gurus seemed to have materialized out of nowhere. Most either started selling on Amazon very recently or aren't selling on Amazon… at all. In some cases, these people have watched my YouTube videos, and have attempted to create copy-cat videos under their own names. They are not experts and they're not actually practicing what they preach, so to speak. If these supposed experts can't show proof of recent, substantial online sales… why would you listen to their advice about selling on Amazon? Would you take financial advice from someone with no track record of profitability and no proof of success in investing? If I want to improve my skills or knowledge in an area, I seek advice only from people who are more knowledgeable and more experienced than I am. It's the only reasonable course of action. In the scam riddled world of online marketing—the way to avoid getting taken is to insist on seeing proof that there is value in a method and that a strategy works as advertised.

Secondly, many of these supposed gurus have little experience (or in some cases, no experience), in actual online selling. I've been selling online for nearly ten years. I started making over $2,000 a month selling socks on eBay when I was in middle school. (In Chapter 2, I'll tell you exactly how I got started selling online.) At the writing of this book, I've been selling on Amazon for five years, using similar principles to the ones that I used on eBay and Craigslist before I began selling on Amazon.

In the month of August 2019, I sold $484,504.28 of goods on Amazon. I sell on Amazon every single day, and I will continue to do so for as long as Amazon is in operation. Even if Amazon were to fail one day (which is very unlikely), I would just move on to the next online selling platform that replaces it.

Sales Summary   •••
Last updated 8/14/19 10:07:51 PM PDT

	Ordered product sales	Units
Today	$22,585.31	1,123
7 Days	$122,425.95	6,060
15 Days	$245,797.64	12,032
30 Days	$484,504.28	23,753

View more of your sales statistics

Another way that I distinguish myself from these other online sales teachers: I'm authentic.

Did you know that many online sales "gurus" fake their screenshots?

I learned recently that it's quite easy for them to create these fakes. On my YouTube channel, I posted a video that explains how these imposters create these bogus screenshots, and, also in that same YouTube video, I actually refresh my account multiple times to show you proof of my recent sales.

Of course, I can't guarantee your personal success. That will depend upon the amount of action you take. But I can give you the tools you'll need to create your own success.

By the time you're done reading this book, you'll know how to:

- Find hidden, authorized suppliers who stock in-demand, well known, and trusted brand-name products

- Set up your business so that you present a legitimate looking image to suppliers and to Amazon (even if you're a twenty-year-old *kid,* like me)

- Analyze suppliers' product catalogs to calculate ROI and profits (after accounting for Amazon fees and competition)

- Automate your business so that it grows while you sleep

Before we dive into the specifics of my methods, I'm going to tell you how I learned and developed all the techniques that I use. You stand to get the most out of the system I've created when you understand the principles behind my strategy.

My approach is straightforward, but the path I took to develop it was complex and took many years to complete. The first steps down that path started around the time that I was twelve years old—and it all started with a pair of socks.

It takes half your life before you discover life is a do-it-yourself project.

— Napoleon Hill

Chapter 1

Why You Should Sell on Amazon

Freedom.

Freedom has been the theme of my life these past few years, as I've scaled my Amazon business.

This past summer, I traveled to Europe for three weeks. The trip was pricey, but during the first four days that I was there, I profited enough in my Amazon business to fund the entire three-week excursion. Basically, I got paid to go to Europe. I made money while on vacation! With my Amazon business, I can travel as much as I want, whenever I want, while I'm still able to watch my bank account grow, even when I'm far away from home.

Sound appealing?

I can manage my Amazon business from anywhere, via my phone or laptop.

I have friends who are now selling on Amazon. My Dad is now selling on Amazon. To date, I have taught my system to over 4,000 people. You'll get a chance to read some of their success stories in Chapter 14 of this book.

Once you've learned how to implement my system, you can operate your business from anywhere in the world, assuming you have access to an internet connection. You can even make money while you sleep. I'll teach you how to automate your business, which will save even more of your precious time.

I've spent the last eight years becoming an expert in selling on Amazon. In this book, I will share that invaluable expertise with you. You'll have all the information, tips and guidance you'll need to get started selling on Amazon. You'll have the tools you need to find your own suppliers. With Amazon's 480,000 item catalog and $31.88 billion in third-party sales, there is plenty of opportunity for all of us to profit. Most Amazon sellers are not aware of the kind of inside information that I will share with you in this book. Having this specialized knowledge will give you a competitive edge over other sellers.

The questions are, first, can you dedicate at least ninety minutes per day to your Amazon business, and second, can you invest a minimum of $1000 to get your business started? Along with reading this book, those are the personal resources you'll need in order to start making money selling on Amazon, within just weeks. This is not a get-rich quick scheme. The amount of money you'll earn in the very beginning may not be life changing. However, it shouldn't take long for you to see significant results, and you'll be able to scale your business as quickly as you can generate the capital needed to reinvest. I've had students who have hit five-figure sales within their first month of business. Then, there are others who never sell a single product—because they never take any action to get things started.

When you sell online using FBA, Amazon handles all logistics, shipping and customer service so that they can guarantee customer satisfaction. Expectedly, Amazon charges you for all these services, however the preferential treatment you receive when using FBA is almost always worth the cost, as long as you price items at the Buy Box market price. (We'll explore the Buy Box in detail in Chapter 11.) Your brand-name products will show up automatically when one of Amazon's 310 million customers does a search, looking for your product type. Brand-name products have the product descriptions and reviews that customers are accustomed to seeing, and Amazon will rotate the sales for the product equally amongst all sellers. Amazon doesn't care who is providing the brand-name product. It could be the brand itself, or some huge store, or a twenty-year-old kid in Washington in his pajamas (me)... or, it could be you. You don't have to do any branding, writing or advertising. You'll simply get a portion of the sales. Shoppers get the product in perfect condition, with two-day Prime shipping. Amazon is so massive and efficient, it's able to provide these perks and conveniences, consistently. They are the best in the world at shipping, infrastructure and overall logistics.

Fortunately, all of this means that you are left with one main job: sourcing.

Sourcing means finding legitimate, brand-name products from authorized suppliers at prices that allow you to get at least 10 percent ROI per month, even after you incur Amazon's fees. Your suppliers will ship your items to Amazon for you. You'll never have to see or touch any products. You can place a bulk order either by phone, email, or online, from anywhere in the world. Your supplier and Amazon will handle everything else. Then, your share of the profits is sent to your bank account. It is that simple.

Ultimately, it is simple, but... there are several things you must learn in order to execute this strategy well.

To give anything less than your best is to sacrifice the gift.

— Steve Prefontaine

Chapter 2

My Story

I'm writing this on a Monday afternoon. I've been in Denver for the week. I travel around a lot, and I'm currently in the process of buying a place in Las Vegas. Mondays are always my busiest day of the week, because, although suppliers get deals over the weekend, those suppliers only available to me Monday through Friday. For that reason, Monday is the start to my week, the day when my suppliers present me with new opportunities.

On this particular Monday, I got up at 9:00 a.m. Mountain Time, and checked my email. Next, I downloaded spreadsheets I'd received from suppliers and ran them through my analyzer tool. My Crabill Analyzer Software Tool is a web-based software that streamlines the process of selecting products from suppliers. In this business, you either get deals from suppliers sent to you one-by-one, or the deals get sent in a long spreadsheet format. If sent in a long spreadsheet, I use my software to analyze the information because it can research **over 50,000 products in under five minutes**. Within thirty minutes, I had determined my order: $10,000 worth of laptops, $1,500 worth of video games and $2,000 worth of electronics accessories. Within an hour and a half, I had called the supplier, placed the order and entered the shipment information on Amazon.

By 10:30 that morning, I was done working on my Amazon business for… the whole week. I had calculated that my ROI would be

37 percent. With one and a half hours of effort, I made $5,000. The supplier immediately got to work shipping my order to Amazon. Amazon would then handle everything else. The products would be shipped to happy customers, and that $5,000 would go into my bank account. (Amazon pays me every two weeks.)

With ninety minutes of work, I made $5,000 in profits. My inventory would be sold within a week—at which point, I could spend another ninety minutes to repeat the process all over again.

But… let's rewind a bit, so that I can show you exactly how I got to the level of success I'm experiencing today.

The reason that I have over ten years of online selling experience already—at just twenty-one years of age—is due in part, to my father. When I was nine years old, my Dad was a small business owner who made extra cash by selling on eBay. At the time, I was trying my hand at entrepreneurial activities typical for an elementary-school kid. I had a lemonade stand, sold arts and crafts, hustled at garage sales.

Seeing my motivation, my Dad decided to get me involved in some of the business that he was doing at the time. He taught me the basics of selling on eBay, such as; how to create a listing, how to post pictures and how to get people to buy your stuff. I helped him with his eBay business for a few years, during my after-school hours… but I never really considered selling anything all on my own.

I kept looking for new ways to make my own money. With my lemonade stand days behind me, I had moved on to a real job—making $5.00 a day cleaning up the dog poop from my neighbor's lawn. I managed to save up $80 from this labor.

For every generation, there are always a handful of fads each year that seemingly everyone obsesses over. When I was in the eighth grade, Nike came out with their "Nike Elite Socks," which were just normal socks made with slightly better material, boasting some cool stripes, and a steep price tag. Who knows why, but, those

Nike Elite socks became a must have fad item. They cost $12 per pair—a lot of money for one pair of kid's cotton socks—but all my classmates had to have a pair. At the time that the Nike Elite style hit the market, the socks were available in two patterns only: black with a white stripe and white with a black stripe. However, before too long, Nike came out with two more patterns: blue socks with a white stripe and red socks with a white stripe. My classmates went nuts. The more styles you owned, the cooler you were.

With my newly earned wages in hand, I saw an opportunity in this sock obsession. What if I could somehow make the socks available in an even greater variety of colors, and I could sell my custom designs to my schoolmates for twice the price of the other Nike Elite socks? I saw how desperate my friends were to be at the top of the 'sock game', so to speak, so, my idea seemed like a no-brainer to me. I decided to invest all my poop job savings into my new business venture. I bought six pairs of Nike Elite socks for a total of $72. Then I used my remaining $8 to buy a few bottles of fabric dye at Joann Fabrics. I went home, read the instructions for the dye, and created my first custom made socks.

To give credit where credit is due, I learned the process of dyeing socks from my friend, Maddy, who showed me how she was dyeing her Nike socks different colors. However, she had done the craft just for fun, whereas I pretty much took that same idea, and turned it into a business. Maddy and I are great friends to this day. (Maddy, if you are reading this—thank you.)

After successfully completing the dyeing process, I went to school armed with my custom sock selection. I had one light blue pair, two purple pairs, one red pair with a black stripe, and two sets that were black and yellow. I sold them all, every pair, immediately, and at a price of $25 per

pair! In very little time, my $80 investment had made me $150— my first real business success. My school friends went crazy over my product and everyone wanted to know where I had gotten the socks. Seeing the demand for my merchandise, I decided to continue making as many pairs of custom socks as I could, so that I could make as much money as possible.

I realized I could purchase the plain socks for less, if I bought them in bulk. I found coupons for bulk sock orders online from Foot-Locker.com. My dad let me use his credit card to place a $150 order (15 pairs of socks), but I had to repay him with my hard-earned cash, on the spot. Empty pockets once again. The next day, I told the kids at school that I could get more of the socks for them, and I took pre-orders. I sold out of my new stock immediately, turning my $150 into $375 almost immediately. I kept repeating the same process and scaled my proceeds up to $1,200. I was on top of the middle school world!

Until I got called into the principal's office.

[School Principal] "Beau, you can't go around selling merchandise on campus and collecting money on school grounds."

Bummer.

Instead of complaining about having my thriving sock business shut down, or feeling sorry for myself, I thought, "How else could I make money with my sock business?" At first, I continued selling a few more pairs to some kids that lived in my neighborhood, but the reality was, I was a twelve-year-old kid, without a phone. I cold-messaged my schoolmates on Facebook and made a few more sales, but it wasn't as easy nor as lucrative as selling directly to my friends at school. Still, I recognized that if the kids at school had loved the socks that I'd made, it was likely that kids all around the country probably would too, right?

It was at this point that I used what my father had taught me about selling on eBay. I listed the socks on eBay for the same $25 price. I had nothing to lose, so why not give it a try? Within a few weeks, I had made a couple thousand dollars in sales. I was blown away by this success and realized the incredible potential in selling online. The only thing that held back my sales was the time it took to manufacture the dyed socks. I was a one-man sock-making show, dying the socks, dipping them in vinegar so that the dye wouldn't fade, then drying them in the dryer, and so forth.

I got more creative too. I kept playing around with design ideas. My next design idea was to turn the white stripes on the black socks into rainbow patterns. This sock style was so unique, that I decided to list them for $36. Immediately, I was selling about four to five pairs per day of the custom rainbow stripe socks. Honestly, I couldn't believe it.

Within two months, I had done over $10,000 in sock sales and had profited about $6,000. It was around this time that Nike expanded their designs to a greater variety of colors and patterns. (Someone at Nike must have stumbled upon my ingenious designs, right?)

Regardless, I didn't give up. I realized I could order in bulk from Nike online, where I was able to get the socks for around $10 per pair. Then I could list those same socks on eBay for $25.00 per pair. I was able to do this because this item was a limited-edition product, and in certain parts of the country it was difficult to find in stores. Online shoppers were willing to pay a premium when they found my merchandise on eBay because they couldn't find the socks in stores in their area. I tested my theory with an order of ten pairs of socks. I sold out quickly, making almost $100 in profit!

At the time, I had no idea that what I was doing had a name, but it's called retail arbitrage. Retail arbitrage is a business model where you source products from retail outlets and then turn around and sell those items at a higher price, online. I was hooked. I determined that I had to figure out how to make the most money possible, selling products online.

The summer after my Nike sock success, I dove deep into retail arbitrage, which, at the time, I just viewed as hustling. I visited a Ross Dress For Less store and began flipping cheap clothes on eBay. Soon, I was making anywhere from $200 to $500 each week. I loved the feeling of success. Funnily enough, Ross often sold

Nike Elite socks for $6 a pair. I wish I had discovered this earlier in my sock business venture. Still, the Nike socks wound up being a best seller for me on eBay as well. Any time I could find them at Ross, I could list and sell them for $12 a pair on eBay.

With a strong desire to keep growing my business, I soon moved on to the next online sales platform: Craigslist. Their barter section seemed to me to have a lot of potential. I went out and bought a pair of purple, Kobe 5 shoes for $50, at a Nike outlet store. I cold-messaged hundreds of people on Craigslist to find the best possible offer for my Kobe 5 shoes. I had to figure out how I could turn my $50 purchase into something of significantly greater value.

First, I traded my outlet Kobe shoes for a newer pair of shoes. I then traded those shoes for a G Shock Watch, which I traded for a PlayStation Portable gaming system (PSP). Traded the PSP for a guitar. Traded the guitar for a speaker system. And, finally, traded the speaker system for a relatively new iPhone 4S, which was the newest iPhone at the time (and the first model to have Siri). I posted this iPhone on eBay and sold it for $425 in profit. This entire process took a few weeks and required sending hundreds of messages, but, again, the overall success felt good.

At this same time, I was spending hours scouring clearance outlets, retail store sales, garage sales, and Goodwill outlets, for good deals. I bought things that I knew were in demand. Brand names. Everything sold quickly. I would even find deals on Craigslist and immediately flip those items on eBay. The strategy was simple, but incredibly effective, and I kept scaling up and up.

When I reached the ninth grade (yes, we're only to the ninth grade at this point in my story), I realized I could buy things from China very cheaply, then, apply my own brand name to these items, and flip them on eBay. I started by buying Kendama toys—Japanese yo-yos. I bought them for about a dollar and sold them for $9.99 on eBay. That went well for a while, and then I branched out to selling cellphone cases. It was my first foray into private labeling—which, frankly, was a much less competitive venture back then and much easier to do than it is today.

With my private labeling business, I quickly started making over $2,000 a month. As a freshman in high school, importing 500 little Japanese toys to my house seemed kind of funny, but, more importantly, it was lucrative. The following year—my sophomore year of high school—my friend Jared's dad heard about my sales activities and invited me out for a sushi dinner. He told me that he was selling Chinese-made headphones on Amazon. It was a great business for him, and he convinced me that the products I was selling on eBay could be sold on Amazon as well. He explained that it would take relatively little effort on my part to sell on Amazon, and I'd get increased demand for my products. It sounded like a perfect opportunity.

On his suggestion, I expanded my eBay arbitrage business and started selling on Amazon also. I sold the same items that I had been selling already, and followed the same strategy, and my profits jumped up!

Then, I discovered Chinese companies that would dropship random items to customers. I sold any cheap and in-demand products that I could get my hands on—products like yoga mats, video games, and presidential coins. From dropshipping alone, I was receiving checks from Amazon for over $10,000, every two weeks. Unfortunately, as well as I was doing with this strategy, it wasn't scalable. I had to find new products every time my inventory sold out. My business required a great deal of my time.

Then, one of my Chinese suppliers told me that he had a few products that I could white label. At the time, I didn't even know what it meant to white label something. I learned that it meant that he would dropship the products to customers, as before, but he would remove the original brand name, and replace that brand with my own brand. The margins with this strategy were huge! (And, yes, this is legal.)

I decided to focus on white labeling, and I profited $35,000 from this strategy within a couple of months.

Meanwhile, my arbitrage business was booming as well. Nike is a restricted brand, but Amazon considered my account in good-standing, and continued to let me sell Nike's products. So, I kept on hustling over to Nike outlets, buying more Nike items, and continued my retail arbitrage business on Amazon.

Things seemed to be going well. I remember one especially momentous moment, when I went out for my regular 8-mile run. When I got to the end of my run, I used my phone to check on my sales. I had sold $3,500 worth of product during that 55-minute period. I had felt that my business was doing well already, but this new mark brought things to another level. It was the result of a combination of Amazon and eBay sales, along with others from Bonanza and from eBid (which I had ventured into as well). To be honest, I was freaking out at that moment. Using my cellphone calculator, I realized that if I could achieve that sales figure in that 55-minute timeframe, once a day, I'd make $1.2 million in sales, that year.

That became my goal.

However, just as quickly as I had decided on this new plan, I received a devastating email from Amazon.

My account was being suspended.

I had no idea why Amazon had done this!

I checked my account: no messages, no warnings, no negative reviews. There were no obvious problems or issues besides a few unfulfilled dropshipping orders. (I had been selling so many items that I must have forgotten to fulfil a few orders.)

Amazon's only message stated that there was a "copyright infringement claim" for my Nike Elite socks. I relaxed a little bit with that clarification. The socks weren't fakes, so, I had nothing to worry about, I thought. I uploaded my receipts from the Nike outlet, intending to prove that the product that I had sold was the real deal. No big deal, right?

A day later, Amazon responded with a message stating that my receipts weren't "validated invoices." I had no idea what that meant. At the time, I didn't even fully understand what an invoice was. To make matters worse, at around the same time, my eBay account was shut down. It turned out that the headphones I had been drop-shipping were cheap knockoffs and the product was not living up to what had been promised to the customer. I was forced to refund over $20,000 and had to change my strategy, completely.

Amazon's customer service was mainly automated, and email based. I couldn't get an answer on how to reinstate my account. I even resorted to emailing Jeff@Amazon.com every day (Jeff Bezos's email account, obviously). Nothing. No response.

Meanwhile, I was still making some sales on eBid and Bonanza, that is, until my PayPal account got shut down too.

Suddenly, I was making zero dollars a day, while, at the same time, becoming obligated to give money back to customers who were making returns. Due to my suspended account status, both Amazon and eBay were withholding money that I was owed, stating that I wouldn't receive those funds for another 90 to 180 days. For the first time in my young entrepreneurial life, I was losing money. I had no idea how to fix this problem, either. I wasn't even completely sure what I had done wrong. It was a total disaster.

Finally, I managed to get a live person at Amazon on the phone. The Amazon representative explained that Amazon didn't accept retail receipts as proof, and that I had to send evidence that I had purchased the items from an authorized supplier.

Keep in mind, I was only a teenager at this point. I had no idea what this Amazon representative was talking about. Nonetheless, I thanked the customer service employee, hung up the phone, and vowed that I would figure it all out. After that Amazon call, I got eBay on the phone. Their customer service was great. I hounded the representative with questions, trying to figure out what their top sellers were doing (that I wasn't doing.) Honestly, I didn't find out all that much in the way of valuable information, but I did realize that I needed to figure out exactly how retail worked.

I knew the basic definition of the word retail, but I didn't understand retail as it relates to a business model. After poking around on the Internet, I realized that retail stores like Best Buy, Target, Sears, Macy's, and GameStop... they are all happy to serve as storefronts and provide shelf space for brand-name products. They simply take a cut of these brands' sales. I recognized that I had to figure out how I could legally sell those products.

After a month's worth of research (and some reverse engineering achieved by calling retail stores to ask them where they got their products), I had figured out the retail model. I found a supplier that supplied to GameStop. This supplier had all the video games you could possibly imagine! I found another supplier—that supplied Ross Dress for Less—who offered brand-name products at bargain prices when bought in bulk. I was cutting out the middleman. I was becoming the middleman.

During this process, I realized that I needed to be very friendly to these suppliers. The Ross supplier was extremely helpful, so I built a relationship with the account manager. Even when that manager made the occasional shipping error or some other administrative mistake, I realized the wisest thing to do was just to accept his apology, and eat the mistake myself, so to speak. Apparently, most people that this manager had worked with had not handled matters in the same way that I had chosen to handle them. He was grateful for my understanding and reciprocated the favor by inviting me to an ASD Trade Show. I had no idea what a trade show was, I just knew it was a good idea to accept his invitation.

Through this trade show experience, I learned where suppliers got their products. It turned out that the Ross supplier bought huge quantities of products from other, even bigger suppliers, who bought in even larger quantities, directly from brands. Beginning with the manufacturers, there were many links in this supplier 'food chain', and along each additional link in the chain, prices went up until they finally reached the last link, the consumer. Even with all the adjustments in prices along the way, each participant in this chain is profitable. The customer pays for the whole process.

Thankfully, the account manager with Ross showed me around the trade show and introduced me to many of the vendors. There were more than 3,000 vendors at this one show. As the supplier taught me the basics of retail, all I kept thinking was: What if I could get a tiny slice of this pie, and leverage it online? As soon as I left the convention in Las Vegas, that's exactly what I started working on. I started working with some of the suppliers I had met—authorized suppliers—and I started selling their brand-name products **legally**, on Amazon. Now Amazon was happy with me, and my business was scalable and sustainable as well.

I still had many important lessons to learn, however.

Such as, suppliers have something called minimum order requirements. Also, for the first time, I was ordering product in bulk. That came with increased risk. Plus, my margins were now smaller than what I had grown accustomed to. I was encumbered with huge orders that I was uncertain would sell. I had no idea how to do product research. My undeterred drive to push forward was fueled mainly by the fact that I was a self-assured teen who had never tasted significant failure.

This strategy, which I call Online Retail, is one that I use and teach to this day. But, in the early days of experimenting with this kind of strategy, I made plenty of mistakes.

For instance, one of my initial suppliers offered to sell me some coffee makers for $110 apiece. He showed me that they were selling on Amazon for $265 each. They did seem to have huge demand (according to their Amazon sales rank), and the profit margin was huge. So, I got excited about their potential profit and ordered close to 300 units (spending $30,000 up front).

How could I lose?

Well, how I lost was… shortly after I bought the coffee makers, the price on Amazon dropped down, down, and down again.

It wasn't until a month after I had suffered this very tough loss that I found a tool called Keepa. Keepa shows you the price history of products on Amazon. Using this tool, I checked the coffee makers and realized that they were being sold for $260 only on that one day that the supplier sent the deal to me! Every other day, the coffee makers were being sold for $150. So, it ended up that after shipping costs and Amazon fees, I barely broke even on that deal. Someone had manipulated the price for that one day. I had been scammed. If I had known the truth of the matter, I never would have bought the product in the first place. Unfortunately, I made other similar mistakes over the next few months. Without any teacher or mentor to guide me, I was stuck having to learn my lessons the hard way.

Fortunately, though, each time I ran into a problem, I did end up finding a solution. It was frustrating to fail, but I worked my way out of each dilemma, and, there were always more products to sell—to get things moving in a better direction again. With time, and a little more experience, I made fewer and fewer mistakes. Soon enough, I was making some serious cash. Overall, the entire learning process took years and had me (almost) hitting rock-bottom, but all my experience allowed me to develop a legitimate and effective business model. Furthermore, I realized it was a model that any person could replicate.

It has been five years since I attended that ASD trade show. Ever since that experience, I've been reinvesting almost all my profits back into my Amazon business, scaling it up while I've learned the mechanics of selling on Amazon and while keeping on top of all the updates to Amazon's algorithm and policies.

I realize that, had I not gotten suspended by Amazon for accidentally breaking their rules, I might not have learned the right way, the best way, to do things. I might have just fumbled around—merely attempting to sell private-label products—wasting my precious time and taking unnecessary risks with my money by spending it on branding and marketing.

Fortunately, I'm here to be your mentor and teacher. I'll teach you how to avoid those mistakes that I made in my early days—days when I had no one to rely upon other than myself.

By the time I was in the ninth grade, I was making more money than all my teachers. (I kept this fact to myself.) Amazingly, I was still treating my Amazon and eBay businesses like side hobbies, really. I kept my focus on school, my friends, and my family, and I was able, still, to make significant profits in my online sales businesses, with relatively little time commitment on my part.

Then, during my sophomore year in high school, I joined the track and cross-country teams, where I quickly excelled to a high-level runner. Running was something I'd always enjoyed, but I had never understood my full potential in the sport, until I started running competitively at school. This led me to decide to focus on my running activities. With this decision, the sport began to consume more and more of my focus and energy, and I decided to dedicate my attention to running cross-country and to running track at the Division 1 college level. As running became a more serious and time-consuming component of my life, I began spending less and less time on my businesses.

Heading into my junior year of high school, my running success had reached a plateau. I had relied on my natural athletic abilities to get me through practices and racing to this point. Although I knew I could run at an even higher level, I lacked the necessary training and knowledge that was needed in order to succeed in running at a Division 1 level. I decided to reach out to some runners who were performing at a much higher level than I was. I got in touch with well-known local runners, college runners, and award-winning high school runners in neighboring cities as well. After considering all the advice I had gathered from these athletes, one fact stuck out: I needed to run more. On average, I was running about 15 to 25 miles per week. I soon realized my current output wasn't even remotely close to the mileage that I needed to cover each week, in order to reach my goal of competing successfully at the college level.

As my motivation increased, my weekly mileage increased as well. My previous running maximum of 25 miles per week turned into 40 miles per week, and then 40 miles became 60, and then 80 miles per week. Less than one year before this, running 100 miles in a week would have seemed like an impossible achievement to me. Now, here I was, thinking 100 miles was just a good week of training. With my eyes set on attaining a college scholarship, I began my junior track season feeling confident and well trained.

On a warm Saturday in April, my team traveled to North Thurston High School in Lacey, Washington, for a highly anticipated meet. For most of my teammates, this event was just like any other competition. For me, however, it was a chance to prove myself against a rival top runner.

North Thurston's top runner, Peter Allegre, was a friend that I had trained with during the Summer. We had become good training partners by this point. However, whenever Peter and I were in competition with one another, the friendship was more or less suspended. Towards the end of this meet, Peter and I were to face off in the two-mile race event. It was scheduled as the last race of the day. The race was highly anticipated. As the event drew near, I was feeling more and more confident. I was convinced that I could win the race and beat Peter.

Seconds after the starting gun sounded, Peter and I were already yards ahead of the rest of the pack. I held position right behind him and kept pace. The first mile felt amazing. As the last three laps approached, I made my move. I pulled out in front of Peter and stayed out in front—up until the point that he and I reached the last two-hundred-yard stretch of the race. As I came around the final corner, Peter flew passed me and won the race with a time of nine minutes and thirty-one seconds. This race ended up being the deciding factor for Peter's scholarship offer from the University of Portland. I was devastated to have come in second place. However, my race time of 9:36 was only seconds away from a Division 1 runner. My hopes were high, still.

The following week, I posted a 4:22 mile time in a midweek meet. I felt like I was on top of the world. Within days, my own college offers started to pour in. I got offers from the University of Washington, University of Portland, San Francisco, Pepperdine—all great schools—I felt sure that my college aspirations were about to come true. After a lot of careful consideration, some deliberation with my Dad, and many phone calls with the coaching staff, I accepted a Division 1 scholarship at Pepperdine University near Malibu, California. My dedication to running had secured a scholarship after all, and a spot on a college running team was finally in my near future. I decided to spend even less time on my online businesses at this point. I was spending as little as 15 minutes a day on eBay and Amazon orders, and that little bit of time was spent packaging orders and quickly checking my sales.

As my junior year was ending, most of my energy was invested in running. If I wasn't running, I was thinking about running, taking a nap to recover from a run, eating to run later, or, I was sleeping.

During the summer leading into my senior year, I was running faster than ever before, and I was in the best physical shape of my entire life, and college life was just a short school year away.

One late summer day, I went to the football field to do some barefoot strides. After finishing those, I drove straight to the gym. At the gym, I put on my shoes, took two steps, and immediately felt sharp pain shooting through my Achilles tendon. When a serious injury occurs, you instinctively know that it is bad, and a sinking feeling of having suffered a bad injury came over me instantly.

Despite the sharp pains, I tried to tell myself not to get upset, not to overreact. I simply left the gym and drove back home and iced my leg immediately. In my head I was telling myself, this is nothing.

I woke up the next day, put my shoes on… and then, couldn't make it three steps.

Something was wrong. Very, very wrong. Immediately, anxiety overwhelmed me. I can't be injured, I thought, I have to be able to run.

Panicked thoughts raced through my mind. What if I lose my scholarship? What if I can't recover completely? What would I do about college if I can't run?

I decided against trying to run that morning. This would be the first day during the entire summer, that I took a break from taking a morning run. That afternoon, I went to practice and told my coach about the Achilles issue. For the first time since my junior year, I took an entire day off from running.

The following day was the day before what would be the first race of the year. I did a short two-mile run with the team, our typical regimen before a race. My Achilles tendon felt better than it had, but it still didn't feel right.

On the day of the race, I went about my usual routine, which consisted of not talking to anyone at all, not eating anything, and nervously awaiting the start of the race. My Achilles still felt horrible and I considered not racing. However, I felt like I had done too much work over the entire summer, to forfeit the race. My coach argued against my position and reminded me that there was still the remainder of the season to consider. I negotiated with him and we came to an agreement that I would take part in the race but would take it easy. The plan was for me to use the race as more of a workout.

I didn't warm up for the race, and I didn't even wear my spikes. As I started out, I felt like I was jogging, but I ended up running the

5k distance in 16:06, managing to shave 30 seconds off my previous race time. After the race, I decided that I needed to figure out exactly what was going on with my Achilles. My friend's father was a podiatrist, so I decided to start by getting his assessment. Unfortunately, even after an evaluation and x-rays and scans... we struggled to determine the nature of the injury.

In the end, the conclusion was that my knee was out of place and that my Achilles was compensating for this knee misalignment. Running eighty miles per week on wet and slanted Washington roads had caught up with me. I had run so many miles on rough and slippery roads that it actually changed the way that I walked. The doctors suggested that I take a full week to rest and recuperate completely, and then spend time using crutches to help support myself while walking. A week later, I was back up and getting around on crutches at school and teaching myself how to walk properly again.

Honestly, I felt embarrassed to see my teammates, embarrassed to see my coach, embarrassed to have to explain to my friends why I couldn't run. I decided to take a full week off school to rest and to adjust to my injured state. Stuck at home, I felt depressed and hopeless. I would go to bed early because I did not want to talk to anyone in my family. I felt embarrassed to have to face my Dad when he'd come home from work. While isolating myself in my room, I spotted a book on my desk that I had gotten for Christmas. The book was, Laws of Success, by Napoleon Hill. My father had given it to me as a present, but I hadn't bothered to read it because—it had nothing to do with running.

I began reading, and I was hooked immediately. I read until I fell asleep.

I woke up the next morning, said goodbye to my dad as he left for work, and, not wanting to waste any time, picked up the book again. I finished reading the whole thing around six o'clock that same evening. The book's message had a profound impact on me. I felt extremely motivated and I felt like I'd figured out what I wanted to do with my life. The most important principle I gained from that book was that taking action, with a concentrated focus on a specific vision, leads to success. Around eight o'clock that night, I went into my small home office where I packaged and shipped out products for eBay and Amazon. As I was packing up products to mail out, I had a light bulb moment. I realized that this was something that I was really good at—making money by selling products online. This is it. I knew I should be focusing on this one thing, and that I had to begin taking action in order to grow this business into a full-fledged profession.

I decided that all the time and energy that I had been investing in running and athletic training, was now going to go into growing my business. Instead of focusing on running, or just hanging out with friends on weekends, I quickly grew my business to over $30,000 per month in sales. (I eventually got my sales up to $60,000 per month before I graduated high school.)

This transition and growth spurred both by the unexpected change in my athletic pursuits and the reading I'd done during my forced rest time, was the catalyst for the subsequent idea to begin teaching others about my business strategies. This all happened during the spring of 2017. Amazon sales gurus were popping up all over You-Tube at that time. I'd watch their videos and come away thinking: What the hell are they talking about? It was clear, to me, anyway, that most of these so-called gurus had never been in the trenches of Amazon selling, so to speak, or, at best, they might have had a little experience with Amazon selling. Most of the advice they gave was horrible and worthless. Some of it may have worked for a small-scale operation, but their strategies would not work for the average person. Without hesitation, I decided to start making videos that refuted the advice I was hearing on these other YouTube channels that were preaching arbitrage, dropshipping and private labeling. I made my videos with the intention of explaining why these methods weren't smart for the average person to undertake.

My YouTube channel grew quickly. People started reaching out to me, asking for coaching or for an online course. My immediate response to these inquiries was to say that I didn't provide that sort of thing and had no plans to start offering those kinds of services. As I was building my YouTube channel, I was getting healthy again, physically. Pepperdine still offered me the scholarship even though I did not race once during my senior year of high school. With that offer, I decided to sign an NLI (National Letter of Intent). I was still going to college. I would be going to Pepperdine to become a top runner, nationally. I was assuming that, once I got to Pepperdine and would have to focus on classes, training, and races, I wouldn't have enough time left over to continue working on my YouTube channel. In the meantime, the more videos I made, the more requests I got for sales coaching. I mentioned this to my Dad, and he insisted that I give teaching or coaching a shot. "Just see if you can help them," he said. Remembering what I'd read of Kiyosaki's and Hill's advice, I felt I should give it a try, at least.

In the beginning, I worked one-on-one with a small number of people. Right away, they saw results from the lessons I shared with them. For me, however, this new venture became overwhelming, quickly. I was soon spending eight to nine hours each day, working with my newfound students—and this was in the middle of the same pre-college summer where I was running over ninety miles per week as part of my training and preparation for attending Pepperdine. It became obvious to me that I couldn't continue to spend eight hours each day coaching my online sales students. This realization led me to create an online course.

At the same time that I arrived at Pepperdine, I was finalizing the creation of my online course. I knew that trying to balance my running and training and my academic load would be tough, but I had no idea how much more time-consuming college academics would be compared to my high school coursework. After only a few days at Pepperdine, I recognized there was no chance that I would be able to be a student athlete and continue to run my business. I must forfeit running or quit my business. It was clear that I had to say goodbye to one of my two biggest passions.

While at preseason training camp, I really began to think things over. Five days into camp, I realized the hard truth: As much as I loved running, I couldn't bear the thought of waiting another four years to restart my business. I had come too far with it by this point and I knew the potential it held for success.

It was the hardest decision of my life thus far, but I decided to forgo my scholarship… and to leave Pepperdine.

The decision was gut wrenching. Truthfully, I cried while telling my coach I was leaving.

But I knew I had to bow out of my competitive running, in order to focus every ounce of time and energy on my business pursuits.

A few days later—on August 23, 2017—I launched my online course, and, I've never looked back.

At the time that I dropped out of Pepperdine, my dad was working as a finance manager at a car dealership. Throughout my entire upbringing he had worked his tail off, so to speak. He had always been supportive of my business ventures. I owe much of my success to his guidance. With Dad in mind, I made my first big, post-college-dropout goal: Convince my Dad to quit his stressful day job.

I started toward this goal by teaching him the basics of selling on Amazon, just like he had done for me when he taught me about selling on eBay, almost ten years earlier. He caught on quickly and helped me grow my Amazon business significantly. Soon thereafter, he got out a calendar and marked a day in July. "I'm going to quit my job on July 13, 2018," he said. That happened to be the date of my 20th birthday as well. As it turned out, my Dad quit his job in March of 2018—four months ahead of his goal. Seeing the incredible potential in this business, he couldn't resist starting his own Amazon business, and now he makes his full-time income through his online business (while still helping me with my business and online course as well.)

Just like me, he works on his Amazon business an average of ninety minutes a day, from home. We both communicate with suppliers every day and sell all kinds of brand-name products to people all over the world.

Every day, I teach more and more students to do what Dad and I are doing. I have students and suppliers all over the world—from Australia to Mexico to Canada and China, and all over Europe too.

To give you a clear idea of how well this business is going, the following graphics display real examples of my sales, at the time that this material was being written.

Looking at just one day of sales for this recent month, my sales equaled: $28,182.69.

Date	Sales breakdown	Fulfillment channel	
Today - Sep 18, 2019	Marketplace total	Both (Amazon and seller)	Apply

Sales snapshot taken at September 18, 2019 10:25:12 PM PDT

Total order items	Units ordered	Ordered product sales	Avg. units/order item	Avg. sales/order item
1,137	**1,200**	**$28,182.69**	**1.06**	**$24.79**

For a recent month, my total sales equaled: $484,504.28.

Sales Summary ...

Last updated 8/14/19 10:07:51 PM PDT

	Ordered product sales	Units
Today	$22,585.31	1,123
7 Days	$122,425.95	6,060
15 Days	$245,797.64	12,032
30 Days	$484,504.28	23,753

View more of your sales statistics

Last year, my annual sales equaled over $1.2 million:

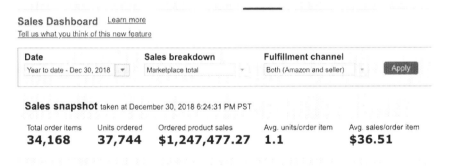

This year, as of mid-September, my sales have reached over $1.9 million already!

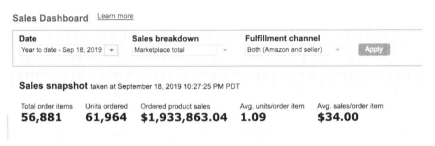

I focus on growing my sales numbers every day—though, much of my business is working and growing while I'm asleep. In addition to growing my own sales, I'm in contact with many of my students (there are thousands of students now), as I work to help bring them closer to their goals as well.

I've helped them succeed.

Now, I'm going to help you.

When you only see problems. You're not seeing clearly.

— Phil Knight

Chapter 3

Three Principles for Success with Selling on Amazon

People in my audiences tend to ask me the same questions, such as: If suppliers have access to products at the cheapest prices, why don't they just sell those products on Amazon themselves? Why don't all brands just open their own brick and mortar retail stores? Why does Microsoft choose to sell to suppliers, who then sell to retailers (e.g., Walmart, Best Buy), who then sell those products to customers?

The short answer regarding the reason suppliers do not sell directly to Amazon is: It just doesn't fit the supplier's business model.

The U.S. retail market is a $6 trillion enterprise. Suppliers and brands have a pretty good gig as it is. Most huge brands and suppliers have been around for decades. Most of the suppliers I work with are doing about $30 million to $100 million in business per year. As massive a business as Amazon is, it accounts for only around 5 percent of that $6 trillion retail market. For a supplier or brand to focus solely on Amazon would mean they'd be ignoring the other 95 percent of their market. They'd rather let the smaller 'players' (like us) handle it—while they take a portion of the sales.

Being a CEO of a wholesale company is not a bad gig, which, is the reason I've turned some of my attention to buying up suppliers. Suppliers are in the business of buying product in massive volumes that they then wholesale to us Amazon sellers. The suppliers make a margin, and we sell the product on Amazon. The wholesalers would rather sell everything in bulk instead of selling things one by one, directly to consumers. Whereas, I'm fine with selling directly to customers because I know how selling on Amazon works and my margins are much better than my suppliers' margins. Suppliers have tons of resources and excellent contacts, so their established business model is their best strategy. Conversely, because neither you (nor I) have the same degree of business history, or resources or extensive contacts that most suppliers have—selling on Amazon is our best strategy.

There is a place for all of us in this enormous, massively profitable industry. The following story will illustrate my point:

I have a supplier who had 2,000 Hasbro Star Wars Lightsabers that he wanted to sell. He could have sold these toys on Amazon himself. There was nothing stopping him from doing that. Some suppliers do have non-compete agreements which means they aren't allowed to sell retail, but that was not the case for my supplier.

By selling to multiple retailers instead, my supplier was able to sell 1,500 units to brick and mortar stores immediately (specifically, to Macy's and Ross Dress for Less.)

What happened to the remaining 500 units that he had? He sold those to yours truly, Beau Crabill, who turned around and sold them on Amazon. I took the data on the Star Wars Lightsabers, ran those numbers through my analyzer tool and determined that it would take six months to sell 2,000 lightsabers. Actually, it took only a couple of months to sell all of them, and I hit my target margin and was very happy with the overall outcome.

Basically, my supplier had a lower margin—but he could sell out his inventory of lightsabers in one day which allowed him to move on to the next product. In comparison, I achieve higher margins, but on lesser volume, and my inventory may not sell out immediately.

Suppliers focus on one thing: Moving product as quickly as possible. They have virtually unlimited access to products. The quicker they sell, the faster they can move on to purchase the next product. Suppliers aren't delayed in their business operation by lack of capital or restricted access to products, in the way that you and I might be in our retail businesses. The supply business has a massive barrier to entry. Simply, it takes an enormous amount of money, time, credibility, established connections, and storage space. You would need warehouse space for operations. Most of the companies I work with have been in business for decades and they have tons of capital.

Brands have a focus similar to that of suppliers, which is, to satisfy and increase the existing demand for their products. However, brands aim to immediately manufacture and send products to suppliers. Suppliers focus on selling that product quickly. Brands focus on creating demand and manufacturing. You and I (and other retailers) focus on getting products into the hands of consumers. In the context of our online sales business, Amazon does most of the work by providing the warehouse space, handling the shipping and managing customer service. Amazon wants us to deal with the suppliers. In the example mentioned above, my supplier could have achieved a higher ROI by selling his product on Amazon, but it would have taken him much longer to move his inventory, and there could have been a possibility that he would not have been able to sell all of his inventory, as well.

Each of us, meaning; Amazon, the suppliers, the retailers, and the brands, we all have different business models, assets and incentives. In Bill Gates' book, Business @ The Speed of Thought, there's an entire chapter called, "The Middleman Must Add Value." The middleman is just a part of business, and they always add value to the next player along the chain. Most of the suppliers that I do business with make 75 to 80 percent of their sales to brick and mortar stores. Often, I'm the only Amazon seller they work with. Occasionally, some suppliers will try to sell on Amazon. When I see that occurring, I avoid working with that supplier, because I'm not interested in buying from a competitor.

In relation to the entirety of brands that exist, a relatively small number of brands do have retail arms as well (e.g., Apple Store). However, even giants like Apple sell outside their own retail locations. A large percentage of their sales are produced via third-party retailers such as Best Buy, Target, Walmart, Sprint… and Amazon. This is great news!

As you'll be getting your products from distributors, this means you won't have to deal with the big brands' CEOs or employees. You get to deal with supplier sales reps who will be enthusiastic to work with you so that they are able to sell their products—products which you will then turn around and sell online for a higher price. Brands are not your competitors, and neither are the suppliers. Both are your teammates, in a sense, and you can get rich by helping them get rich too. It's a mutually beneficial relationship.

Principle Number One: *Patience*

Another question I'm asked frequently is: If my strategy is so simple, why doesn't everyone do what I do?

Truthfully, everyone could do what I am doing. I don't claim to be especially unique or gifted or talented. However, there are plenty of reasons that many people don't do what I do. My method is simple, but that doesn't mean that every person will do what is required to succeed. Also, a seller's business growth rate will be correlated to how much he or she is willing and able to reinvest resources back into their business. This is not a Get Rich Quick scheme. Many people lack the patience, perseverance and work ethic needed to succeed in this business. Some of the people who will read this book, will see the potential in the business, but then will end up getting distracted by some other "shiny object" and they will never get their reseller businesses off the ground. Some students will start their own business selling on Amazon, and will begin to have some success as well, but then will lose motivation and momentum when they can't afford to buy a Ferrari after one year in business.

The substantial profits to be made by selling on Amazon will come in the long term, from compound interest. Yes, I've scaled my business to produce seven figures in sales. Keep in mind, I've been selling online and reinvesting my profits consistently for eight years. This is not overnight wealth. I have reinvested every single dollar that I've made (that I didn't need to maintain my unpretentious lifestyle). I wasn't making millions in my early days, and you won't start off making millions either, most likely.

Compound interest isn't magic, but it can sometimes feel like it is just that. Albert Einstein has been quoted as referring to compound interest as the eighth wonder of the world. Additionally, MarketWatch (a news outlet for financial news), wrote this:

> "Ask Warren Buffett for the single most powerful factor behind his investing success, and he'd respond, 'compound interest', without skipping a beat. He's been preaching this for six decades, and it's made him a billionaire. And it's something every investor can copy."

My strategy incorporates long-term investment. Let's say you begin with $1,500 as product investment in your Amazon online sales business. You begin by finding your first authorized supplier, and then identifying a product that has a 10 percent ROI (after accounting for all of Amazon's fees, as I'll explain in detail in a later chapter). Once you've identified the right product, you buy $1,500 worth of inventory and estimate that it will sell out within a month.

The first month, you'll make $150 in profit.

(Meh.)

But then, you follow my advice and reinvest, including all your profits.

The second month, you'll make $165.

(Still meh.)

After a year of selling on Amazon using this strategy, you'll have $4,707.64.

A little less meh, now. You have more than tripled your investment!

But wait for this.

After five years of selling on Amazon, your $1,500 initial investment will have grown to:

$456,722.46.

That's over 300-times your initial investment!

Imagine if you had more than $1,500 to invest. Or, if you found products that generated a higher ROI than 10 percent (10 percent being the absolute minimum ROI rate that I recommend when selecting products to buy). Suddenly, becoming a millionaire within five years isn't such a farfetched idea anymore. You must take action and have patience. Many people struggle to maintain a balance with this combination of behaviors.

Principle Number Two: Take Substantial, Quick Action

When people ask what differentiates my successful students from my unsuccessful students, my answer is simple: The amount of action each one chose to take. Most people nod in agreement when hearing my response, but I know that they probably don't really get what I'm saying. In reality, most people are not good with follow-through.

If you're an action taker… or if you become one after this wake-up call… you're likely to make mistakes, especially when first starting out. The important thing is that you learn from those mistakes, make corrections, and continue taking action. If you're not one who can learn to make decisions and take action… you'll never do anything! I've created a YouTube video where the whole point of my video was to separate action takers and opportunity seekers…

from mere critics, meaning skeptics. A skeptic views my videos and says, "I'd never listen to someone so young." An action-taker asks, "How is it that someone so young was able to become so successful?"

Remember, I started my business with the $80 I made from picking up dog poop. Now I make seven figures a year selling on Amazon. If you're truly looking for opportunity, you'll find it. No matter what you choose to do, creating opportunity for yourself requires that you take action, plain and simple.

Principle Number 3: Keep Things as Simple as Possible

One reason my strategy is invaluable is that it is unlike all the ineffective sales tactics taught by most of these so-called, "pop-up gurus" that you'll likely encounter on YouTube or other online platforms. Most of these supposed experts will tell you that you need to start your online business by creating your own brand. Even the savviest of entrepreneurs fall victim to that misguided advice. Starting your own brand sounds enticing… but creating your own brand is difficult to do successfully, and therefore, is a very risky venture. Recently, I was consulting for a successful retail store in the Bronx. When I explained my strategy to them, they made it clear that they thought my approach was unsound. Their store had been in business for over twenty years already and they had established great relationships with manufacturers, wholesalers and distributors. They knew the retail business as well as anyone. But they didn't know Amazon like I know Amazon. They came to me because they recognized Amazon's power and could see how fast Amazon was growing and they knew also that brick and mortar stores were closing left and right, unable to compete with Amazon's model.

Surprisingly, here's what these smart, successful Bronx entrepreneurs asked me first:

"How do we create our own brand and how do we market it?"

Creating a brand for oneself, is in opposition to the business strategy that I preach.

I walked around their store and saw big name brands everywhere. Carhartt. North Face. Levi's.

I ran some numbers through my proprietary analyzer software and pointed at a simple Carhartt tee-shirt.

"How many units of these do you sell per month?" I asked.

Retailer, "In a good month, sixty units."

"Amazon sells 8,000 of these per month," I explained. "If you put your existing products on Amazon, simply by using FBA, you could make an extra few million dollars per year, all without the expense of dropshipping or dealing with customer service." "Why spend time and money convincing people to buy some no-name or off-brand pair of shorts… when you can just give them the Nike shorts that they really wanted in the first place?"

Obviously, the company agreed with me. They decided not to create their own Amazon brand.

To me, it was a no-brainer for them to begin selling on Amazon, because they had solid supplier relationships already. By selling on Amazon, they'd benefit from gaining the traffic of millions and millions of Amazon's existing customers.

This store had spent decades establishing their suppliers and sourcing their products. To make their business grow exponentially, all they needed was my insight and to learn my strategy.

To reiterate my approach:

1. Find authorized suppliers who sell in-demand, brand-name products.

2. Analyze their catalogs to find inventory with the best ROI and turnaround time.

3. Buy low from the supplier.

4. Sell (much) higher on Amazon using FBA and my match pricing strategy to win the Buy Box and guarantee sales. (These Buy Box pricing concepts are explained in detail in later chapters.)

To make money on Amazon, all you need to do is learn how to source in-demand products, buy low, and then sell high. In this book, that's exactly what I teach you to do.

Most people think they have to reinvent the wheel in order to sell on Amazon. They think they need to create a private label to compete with big brands (brands which, incidentally, have spent billions of dollars on research and development and on earning market share and who have decades worth of experience and expertise related to branding).

New sellers often think they need to create demand for their own products. In reality, considering the fact that a company like Hasbro spent $269 million on research and development in 2017 alone—it doesn't make any sense for a new seller to try to compete with them.

I sell Hasbro products every day, and every day, Hasbro spends some of their quarter-of-a-billion-dollar annual budget to make sure people continue buying their products. Essentially, Hasbro products, are my products. Nothing is guaranteed in the online sales business, but this type of deal, selling products from a company such as Hasbro, is the closest you can get to a guaranteed win. When you take the credibility of a major brand like Hasbro and add it to Amazon's credibility and customer traffic, you've got the Holy Grail of online business models.

It is important to mention that, even when something doesn't go as planned with your Amazon sales, there are different ways to recoup your investments. If you buy inventory that doesn't sell as expected, you can sell it in different countries (like Amazon Europe, Canada or Mexico), or you can sell it on eBay, or, to marketplaces for big stores like Walmart and Sears (where part of their business model is to buy other people's excess inventory.)

Also, older products sell successfully on Amazon. You may be surprised to learn that there are Barbie dolls—that first came to market ten years ago—that sell well on Amazon. Remember, Amazon has unlimited digital shelf space. There's no reason for them to take a product 'off the shelf' even if it is selling slowly. Brick-and-mortar stores with limited display space do not have this same leeway.

Needless to say—you should be selling on Amazon. Keep in mind that I know practically nothing about marketing. And I know little about branding. You don't need any specialized skills to do what I'm going to teach you to do. You don't need large sums of capital. You don't need to be a genius. I'm not a genius. I'm just smart enough to realize that the best plan is to work with Amazon and the big brands...instead of against them.

Action is the real measure of intelligence.

— Napoleon Hill

Chapter 4

First Steps

Before you begin the process of finding your first supplier, there are some critical prerequisite business planning that you need to implement—the part of this whole process that I refer to officially, as: The Boring Stuff.

All kidding aside, I can't stress enough how important it is that you read the following sections carefully and make sure that you follow the instructional steps accurately.

Be sure to complete all the following steps **before** contacting suppliers or placing orders.

The Prerequisites for Getting Started

I like to recommend that each student starts his or her Amazon business with at least $1,000 (ideally around $2,000), which will be used, in part, to pay for the fundamentals discussed in this chapter. You will need a small amount of capital to buy physical product, as well. If you don't have the money currently, don't worry. This business model is here to stay! Focus on saving your start-up money as quickly as possible and then start whenever you're ready. You may consider selling items around your house using my eBay Course, in order to launch your Amazon business as soon as possible.

Step 1: Set up a legal business

I established an LLC (Limited Liability Corp.), for my Amazon business, and many Amazon sellers choose to go that same route as well. However, I do know many successful Amazon sellers who operate as sole proprietors. Requirements vary by state and by country. Be sure to research the rules that are applicable in your area, and you may wish to consult a tax attorney or other legal advisor to choose the appropriate business structure. Typically, setting up an LLC will require a little paperwork and usually costs around a few hundred dollars. (Operating as a sole proprietor is usually free or may have some very small cost associated with it.) To be very clear, I am not giving any legal business advice here. I suggest that you do some research online to find specifics regarding getting a business license in your place of residence and be sure to follow those regulations carefully. Most of the time, you'll be able to find a government portal online that will give you very clear instructions, and which will provide contact information, should you have any questions regarding what is required. I cannot provide any answers regarding the legal business requirements for your particular area.

> Note: When filling out any form that asks you to describe the type of business that you will be conducting, you can choose "retail e-commerce," or "selling retail online," or something similar. If there is a space provided for Notes, mention that you'll be selling on Amazon (and list eBay, wholesale, or any other method of selling that you plan to do).

The instructions online should be self-explanatory, but here are a few helpful guidelines:

- Your business address can be your home address.

- If you don't want to use your home address, you can search online to find out how to get a "virtual mailbox." Otherwise, you can visit your local UPS store to get a commercial mailbox or go to your local post office to inquire into getting a P.O. Box.

- If you're setting up an LLC, you'll need a business name. Your name choice isn't all that important for our purpose of creating an online sales business. Just choose something appropriate. If you're operating as a sole proprietor, you can just use your own name (but you're not required to). Usually you have the option of using a fictitious name instead.

Step 2: Get your *reseller's permit*

If you live in one of the forty-five U.S. states that has a sales tax, you will absolutely need some sort of permit to resell products. The process of getting this type of permit is usually very simple and inexpensive but it is a **crucial step**, as well. The name of the permit, its cost and the procedure required to procure a permit will vary by state (and by country, of course). The permit might be called a "Reseller's Permit," a "Sales Tax Permit," a "Certificate of Authority," or possibly something similar. Whatever it's called in your area—just get one as soon as possible. The whole process can usually be done online and costs around $25, although I've seen processing costs as low as $5, and as high as $100.

Virtually all suppliers will ask you for your permit information as soon as you contact them. Make sure you have it available, before reaching out to any supplier. Make sure you have a physical copy, a digital copy and the specific permit number safely saved, and a back-up copy saved as well. Suppliers will usually ask that you email a copy of the certificate itself, but that really depends upon the supplier. This permit exists to help you. If you didn't possess one, you'd be entitled to pay sales tax on all the orders that you make with your suppliers. Once you have a permit—you become tax exempt on purchases from suppliers. You'll also be allowed to collect and remit sales tax to your state's department of revenue. By having your permit ready to show to your supplier, you'll immediately signal to them that you're a legitimate entity. Many new

Amazon sellers fail to follow this critical step and then, they aren't taken seriously by suppliers. Don't make that mistake.

If you live in one of the five states that does not have sales tax, be sure to communicate that fact with your supplier. (They may be unaware of this status if they are operating out of a different state that does have a sales tax.) Often, suppliers will ask for some sort of tax identifier number, as well. Technically, this can be your social security number—but it can be helpful to get an EIN for your business. EIN stands for Employer Identification Number otherwise known as a Federal Tax Identification Number. Having an EIN is yet another signal to a supplier that you're a legitimate business, even if you're operating as a sole proprietor. You can search online to find out how to get an EIN in your location. Again, this process can often be done online for free.

Don't let these steps dissuade you from moving forward. This process may seem unfamiliar or daunting when you first encounter all these new stipulations, but it should be relatively easy to research your region's requirements online. Simply follow the rules and procedures for your region and you'll soon be ready to move to the next step.

Disclaimer: I am neither a tax attorney nor an accountant. It is your responsibility to become familiar with the laws that govern your place of residence. Contact an expert in your local area if you feel that you need help with any part of this process.

Step 3: Items and resources you will need when placing your first order

Ideally, it is a good plan to estimate that you will need at least $1,000 to get started when placing your first order.

Virtually all good suppliers will have something called an MOQ (Minimum Order Quantity). This means the supplier won't allow you to place an order for anything smaller than their set MOQ. The lowest Minimum Order Quantity I've seen from a legitimate supplier was $250. Usually, the MOQ is at least $500—and for the best suppliers (the ones with the most profitable products), the MOQ is usually $1,000 or higher. A quick comment on starting small: I know many people who have started with a mere $500 order, who have then been able to sell their inventory quickly—and then reinvest their profit in their next orders—so that they were able to quickly compound their initial small investment. This is absolutely possible to achieve. My point is, don't let a shortage of capital completely deter you from getting started.

Compound interest is the name of the game. Start as soon as you can and reinvest as much as you can afford. Starting today with a $500 order is better than waiting for another six months just to be able to start with $2,000. I make orders for around $500 all the time. There is nothing wrong with a small order, when you're committed to reinvesting and continuing with your business for the long term. Suppliers care most about creating long-term partnerships because it will make them the most money in the long run.

Step 4: Create Your Amazon Seller Central Account

Setting up an Amazon Seller Central Account is very simple. Go online to: www.sellercentral.amazon.com and follow the instructions provided on that site.

The process is straightforward, but I've listed some helpful tips and information here as well:

- If you plan to make more than forty sales during your first month of business (and you can afford the $39.99 monthly fee), sign up for the "Professional Plan." Otherwise, sign up for the "Individual Plan," which is **free**.

  - ➢ Basically, the professional plan provides some extra benefits (as explained in detail on the website). When you use an individual plan, you're charged 99 cents for every item you sell.

- You can sign up using your existing Amazon account, or you can create a new account.

- Don't be concerned about all the information Amazon requests from you. Amazon has top notch cyber security. They need this information from you in order to verify that you're a legitimate business (which, you will be, if you have followed the prerequisite steps in this chapter).

  ➤ For accounting purposes, it usually makes sense to open a business banking account, but the choice is yours. You could start off just using a personal banking account and then, you can change your banking information later, if you decide to open a designated business checking account for your business. Every two weeks, Amazon will deposit any revenues you've generated into whichever bank account you've provided to them.

- For your Tax ID number, you can use your social security number (in cases where you're operating as a sole proprietor), but, if you are operating within an LLC that you've created, you will need to use your EIN (business tax ID number). A sole proprietor can also get an EIN if preferred. (For international students, please follow your country's tax ID procedures.)

- Regarding shipping address: Customers won't see your shipping address and if you're following my strategy and selling FBA, you'll never have anything shipped to your address anyway. When filling out this address information for Amazon, simply use the personal address or virtual address that you've designated for your business. Again, Amazon uses this for verification purposes. Make sure the address you provide is a real address.

- Your "business display name" is what will be seen by customers on Amazon. If you have an LLC, you can, of course, use that name. If you're a sole proprietor—make something up. This choice of names is not particularly important—just choose something that you prefer, and which sounds credible.

- There are a few myths going around regarding Amazon accounts.

  - Myth #1: You can't change your display name after setup.

    - This is not true.

  - Myth #2: Amazon sometimes closes new account registrations.

    - This is also false.

  - Myth #3: You can have only one Seller Account.

    - This is true only when you're first starting out. If you decide to form a second online sales business later, all you'll need to do is contact Amazon to get permission to have a second account.

- Amazon will charge either your credit card or debit card for all Amazon fees. (I'll explain Amazon's fees in detail in later chapters.)

- If you've signed up for an Individual Account, you'll need to present Amazon with a recent bank statement. Again, this is just for verification purposes.

- If you prefer not to use your personal phone number, you can create a "Google Voice" number and any calls to that number will just be forwarded to your personal phone.

Step 5: Explore *Seller Central*

I call Amazon's Seller Central your "back office." It's where you can manage all your Amazon selling activities. All you have to do is visit: sellercentral.amazon.com. You can enter the website from your computer or your smartphone, anywhere in the world that you have Internet access capability.

Seller Central has a lot of complex features, but you need only to become familiar with a few of the features. Most of the time you'll be concerned with the following facets only:

- Tracking shipments from your supplier to Amazon. (You will be double-checking to see that everything is going as planned.)

- Tracking product sales on Amazon. (Again, this is just to ensure that things are going according to your calculations.)

- Tracking the Buy Box prices of your items. If you discover that competitors raise or lower their prices, you may decide to match those prices. This is assuming, however, that you're not repeatedly undercutting one another and thereby ruining sales. (This will be explained in detail in chapter 11.)

- Communicating with Amazon Support if you have any unexpected problems.

As I've explained, this is a very simple business overall. It will not take long to become familiar with and comfortable with using Amazon's Seller Central site.

Here are a few useful tips for navigating the site:

- To **add** a product, scroll/hover over the **Catalog** tab, then click **Add Products**.

- To manage and check **existing inventory**, scroll/hover over the **Inventory** tab, then click **Manage FBA Inventory**. Doing this will display "fee previews" so that you're able to estimate Amazon's cut of your sales, and it will show how much of your inventory is still in stock.

- To manage **pricing**, scroll/hover over the **Pricing** tab, then click on **Manage Pricing**. This will show things like "Buy Box percentage," so that you can ensure that you are indeed sharing the Buy Box fairly.

Lastly, you will see a button to **Automate Price**, but I **don't** recommend choosing this. Keep in mind our strategy: Always match the Buy Box price. (That is, unless another seller gets 'greedy' and keeps undercutting you until you're no longer able to be profitable. In cases like that, be patient. Let that seller sell out of inventory—and then check to see whether the market price returns to the amount that you expected.)

Note: If you ever need to see your account information or change anything on your account, click **Settings** in the top-right corner of your screen. You can refer to Amazon's **Help** section as well.

Price is what you pay. Value is what you get

— Warren Buffet

Chapter 5

Product Analysis

Analyzing Products *and* the Competition

The easiest way to analyze products is by using my Crabill Analyzer Software Tool.

You can analyze inventory manually, but it is a time-consuming method, meaning, it will cause significant delays in your online sales business.

Whichever method or analytical software you decide to use, you'll need to take all the following steps before ordering a product:

1. Find the product's ASIN number (Amazon Standard Inventory Number). This is the number that corresponds to Amazon's listing.

2. Calculate the cost of all Amazon's fees (which includes shipping from your supplier to Amazon). Use Amazon's FBA Revenue Calculator for this calculation which can be found online at: https//sellercentral.amazon.com/hz/fba/profitabilitycalculator.index?lang=en_US .

Evaluating Shipping Costs and Other Fees

Amazon does most of the work for you, so it stands to reason that they are going to charge fees to compensate for all the costs they incur in providing all the services they deliver. The good news is, they're so efficient that the fees they charge shouldn't stop you from finding profitable products. Some of the Amazon fees you'll see, are:

- Referral fees: A percentage of the gross sales on each product you sell on their platform. Generally, this fee will equal between 8 to 20 percent of those sales, depending upon the category. Fees are the same for FBA and FBM.

- Shipping from Amazon: Technically, shipping is "free" when you use FBA. However, you are charged what is termed, "pick and pack fees," and "fulfillment fees," which relate to Amazon identifying your item once it has sold, boxing and packaging it, and then dropping it off to be shipped and so forth. You can consider these costs comprehensively as *shipping fees*.

  ➢ Storage fees: Amazon charges a monthly fee for each item that you store in their warehouses. Storage fees are complicated, because they're based on size, and costs adjust frequently (typically quarter by quarter). You can find *current* storage rates online at: https://sellercentral.amazon.com/gp/help/external/200684750

- Variable Closing Fee: This is a small fee for all media items, like video games, books, and magazines.

Shipping to Amazon

Amazon does charge for shipping that occurs from your supplier to an Amazon FBA warehouse. The price varies, but 20 to 50 cents per item is a good estimated range. I recommend using 50 cents per item as your cost estimate. I've never had a product exceed that cost. We'll discuss shipping logistics further in chapter nine.

After reading this section, it may appear as though you will be getting hit with a lot of fees, but I assure you that you will still be able to find plenty of products with an ROI of at least a 10 percent—even when accounting for these fees.

I looked into shipping and storing things myself or using third party companies to do these tasks—but those options would always end up being more expensive (and would make business more difficult for me). It is better to have Amazon handle these tasks.

Analyzing Price

1. Use Keepa.com to analyze the price history, sales rank and Buy Box history.

   - On Keepa, click on the following options: **New**; **Third-party FBA**; and **Buy Box**, in order to evaluate your competition.

   - Notice what happens when a seller undercuts the price.

   - Do other sellers follow suit and the price settles at that lower mark?

   - Or, does that one seller sell out of product quickly and then over time, the market price returns to a higher price?

   - Is Amazon selling the product themselves?*

   *It is not a problem if Amazon is selling the product, as long as Amazon isn't trying to be the exclusive seller for the product. You can determine whether Amazon is an exclusive seller by checking to see what happens when someone undercuts Amazon's price. Here is what you want to look for:

   ➢ If Amazon *matches the price immediately*—and has the Buy Box most of the time—they're probably trying to be the exclusive seller. In this case, don't compete with Amazon. *You'll lose*. This likely means that Amazon has unlimited inventory for this product, using something called Amazon Vendor Central. (Knowing this term isn't important for our business purposes, but you can research it if you're curious.)

> ➤ *If Amazon hasn't shared the Buy Box in the past, they're unlikely to do so in the future.*

- Convert the sales rank into a monthly sales estimate (by using a tool like AMZScout.net).

- Count the number of Buy Box sellers (including yourself).

If there are no FBA sellers, you can expect to win the Buy Box almost immediately. If an FBM seller still has the Buy Box, just keep lowering your price by a dollar until you win the Buy Box, assuming you remain in profitable position.

- Go to the Amazon listing, click on **other sellers** and count how many sellers there are of *new*, *Prime*, *FBA* products that are selling at the same price—or that are selling *close in price*—it's possible a seller just hasn't matched the price yet but will soon.

- Divide the number of total monthly sales by the number of current Buy Box sellers and any potential new entrants. Include yourself.

For example: If there are currently 4 Buy Box eligible sellers and 100 monthly sales of a product, you can expect 20 sales for yourself. (I.e., 4 sellers + yourself = 5 sellers total; divide 100 sales by 5 sellers = 20 sales for you.)

- There is no limit to the number of sellers who can share the Buy Box.

- Also account for any new *potential* entrants.

> ➤ The only way to determine the possibility of potential entrants is to communicate with your supplier directly.

> ➤ Simply ask your supplier if they know how much more of a product is out in the market with other suppliers.

Your supplier will often know the answer to this question and usually won't mind sharing the information.

- Note: Whenever possible, buy *all* available units. If your supplier deals with other Amazon sellers, assume that all units that you do *not* purchase, will go to your competition.

Calculate your Turnaround Time

Most sellers focus exclusively on ROI. That's a mistake.

You may find one product with a 50 percent ROI and another with a 100 percent ROI. However, you still need to account for volume and turnover time.

- For example: If you calculate that your product has a 100 percent ROI and you can sell out $10,000 worth of inventory (volume) in four months (turnover time), your **monthly ROI** is 25 percent.

- If you find another product with a 50 percent ROI, but you can sell out $10,000 worth of inventory in one month, your **monthly ROI** would be 50 percent.

Both products would be good investments, but if you had just enough investment capital to purchase one product only—obviously the second option in this example would be your best choice.

This is a very simple part of the overall analysis, but many people forget to account for this factor.

Calculate your profitability at the average Buy Box price (and ensure that you're still profitable at the absolute lowest, worst-case scenario).

Identify products that meet your investment criteria. I recommend ordering products that have at least 10 percent ROI and a one-month turnaround, especially when you are first starting out in your online sales business.

It's OK to have your eggs in one basket as long as you control what happens to that basket.

— Elon Musk

Chapter 6

The Role of Suppliers

Don't Focus on Finding Products—Focus on Building Supplier Relationships

Most people considering getting into this type of business tend to get preoccupied with the product side of the business. I often get asked the following questions:

- How will I know which products to look for?

- What are the bestselling product categories?

As I've said before, it does not matter *what* you sell. Once you find good suppliers and build solid business relationships with them, so that they give you their best deals, finding profitable products will be *easy*. But that first part, finding good suppliers (and getting them to trust you), can be a challenge when you are first getting started.

Let me give you a real-life example regarding the importance of supplier relationships in this business. I was consulting for a man named Bret, who, initially, failed to appreciate the importance of supplier relationships over product selection.

Bret is a doctor, and his father is a successful entrepreneur and motivational speaker. Inspired by his Dad's entrepreneurial spirit, Bret was motivated to pursue his own entrepreneurial dreams. Also, the stress of being a doctor had become overwhelming and so, Bret started searching for lucrative ways to make a living where he would still be able to find the level of financial success he hoped to achieve, but in a scenario that had significantly less stress than he was experiencing in his medical practice. Bret happened to find my YouTube channel. After watching several of my videos, he figured he could venture into online sales on his own, without my help or any further education. He was a well-educated doctor, after all. He was confident in his own intellect. However, after a few weeks of searching for suppliers on his own, he contacted me and admitted he was struggling to find any good suppliers at all.

I asked how he was conducting his supplier search.

He told me that he was Googling various supplier-related terms. I then asked whether he had run into suppliers with names like Entertainment Earth and Intex. He told me that those were exactly the ones he was working with. I understood his problem, immediately. When you Google terms such as, "Hasbro wholesaler," the suppliers that show up as a result of that Google search are the ones that have invested serious time and money into SEO (search engine optimization). You're not finding the cheapest suppliers, nor the best—you're finding the same suppliers that the average Amazon seller is finding. This kind of supplier will give you a catalog of 20,000 brand-name products, but when you run the numbers on those products, you will realize none of them are worth buying. These suppliers have tons of interested customers contacting them which means that they can raise their product prices to the point that online sellers like us cannot be profitable. Also, many of these suppliers don't even sell brand name products—they sell Chinese knockoffs. China does not have the same sort of copyright laws that we have in the United States. In the U.S., it is illegal for you to sell something like a fake Hasbro product.

Bret invested in my Online Retail course a few days after my phone conversation with him and he went through the section called, Nine Methods of Finding Suppliers. Ten days after buying my course, Bret made his first sales on Amazon. He found **thirty** promising suppliers, ran their inventory through the Crabill Analyzer Software Tool and found a few profitable products that he was interested in. He placed his first orders and sold out of inventory within days.

Your competitive edge is not achieved by finding the best products.

Your competitive edge is built by finding the best suppliers.

Additionally, building good relationships with your suppliers encourages them to send their best deals your way. There is no shortage of good products to sell. Amazon sells over half-a-million different products and the majority of those sales are brand name items. There is, however, a shortage of good relationships between Amazon sellers and suppliers. My suppliers tell me often that they are grateful that I place large orders consistently, and that I pay on time and I treat them with respect. You'd be amazed at the number of retailers that fail to do these simple but critical things. My good business etiquette and the courtesy I show my suppliers are the reasons that I get offered the best deals. Those great deals maximize my profits.

Focus on finding one good supplier first. Concentrate on becoming that supplier's favorite customer. Take the time and make the effort to build a good relationship with your supplier, and you'll reap the rewards again and again. Invest in the relationship and your returns will compound. Understandably, you may have concerns that suppliers won't want your business when you're just starting out in Amazon selling. Keep in mind, suppliers care about one thing above all else and that is; moving their products as quickly as possible. They have a massive amount of a variety of products. They want to sell that product immediately to make room for more. If products are moving quickly, they're making money. If products go unsold, suppliers lose money instead. The point being, suppliers don't really care who they sell to—as long as they can sell their products quickly and make their margins. As a customer, if you buy items quickly and place orders consistently, your suppliers will grow to appreciate you greatly. This fact is true in the short-term picture and in the long-term view of things. Short-term sales are valued by the supplier, but short-term sales are not nearly as valuable as creating a long-term lucrative win-win relationship between supplier and customer.

As a new Amazon Seller, let's assume that you plan to "start small" by setting your first order for the minimum order quantity. A supplier's MOQ will usually be set somewhere between $500 to $1,500. If you explain to the supplier that you want to start small, as a test run, and that you intend to scale up and hope to work with them for years to come—your supplier will want to help you. A supplier will want your comparatively small $500 to $1,500 investment now, because, a successful partnership could then lead to future orders of thousands of dollars, or maybe even millions of dollars, in the long run. You want to build a relationship with them, and, they want to build a relationship with you. If you distinguish yourself to them, setting yourself apart from the hordes of one-off customers they encounter, you will soon become your supplier's "go-to" customer. This is the reason I recommend starting with just one supplier, and then scaling up gradually to working with just a few suppliers in total. By focusing your energy on finding and working with just one good supplier first—you will stand to make more money, due to the more lucrative deals that your supplier will be willing to extend to you. The key to solving the supplier piece of your overall Amazon sales puzzle, is to focus on the quality of your connections, not the quantity.

You won't get a supplier's very best deals right from the start, but the deals you do get should be good enough to launch your business. There are a countless number of suppliers out there, and you can absolutely find one supplier with one profitable product to get your business going. I made over $30,000 selling Apple products last month, and that was not because I'm some kind of genius for thinking Apple products would sell. Most people are aware of Apple's product success. The reason I made so much money in this case, is because my supplier truly appreciates my business and offered me a deal that would never be found on Google. I put in the time and effort to build a relationship with an Authorized Apple

Supplier, and he gives me great deals on Apple products because of my efforts.

Once you find a good supplier, show them that you truly appreciate their business! Their success will be your success. Suppliers are your teammates, not your competition. Without good supplier relationships, you have nothing. With them, you hold the key to success in Amazon selling.

If you double the number of experiments you do per year,
you're going to double your inventiveness.

— Jeff Bezos

Chapter 7

Finding Suppliers

Understanding the Different Types of Suppliers

To prepare for your supplier search, you'll need to learn some fundamental information about the business. There are many different types of suppliers, and it's important to understand those differences, before you set out to find your first one. Knowing this information will help you understand where your products originated and will make it possible for you to ask the right questions of your supplier. This will be critical knowledge when the time comes for you to determine whether you should place an order.

The suppliers you're looking for fall into four categories:

1. Wholesalers

2. Distributors

3. Closeouts

4. Manufacturers

Some suppliers fall under multiple categories. You might run into a supplier that refers to themselves as a closeout company, but which is also a distributor. A distributor is someone who works directly with a brand (i.e., a manufacturer). If you're selling Hasbro products, and your supplier is a distributor—that means the supplier bought those products directly from Hasbro.

(For our purposes here, brands and manufacturers are the same thing.)

When working with **distributors**, you should ask the following questions:

1. Are you the only distributor for this brand?
2. How many units of this product have you sold already?

Basically, by asking these questions, you're trying to determine whether other competitors will be entering the Amazon market. Competition is expected; however, you will want to account for increased competition when calculating your ROI and turnaround time. A closeout company buys the last of the remaining stock from brands, distributors and from other countries as well. They do this because they get large discounts on these products. This is where online retailers, like you and me, will find our best margins.

When working with a **closeout company**, you should ask:

1. Did you buy all available units when you made this order?
2. Are these the last units on the market?
3. Will there be more of these available later?

A *wholesaler* is someone who buys from other distributors, close-outs or liquidators. Basically, a wholesaler is one step further down the food chain, so to speak, from these product sources. When working with a wholesaler, you should ask the following question:

- When you bought this product, did you buy the entire inventory?

  ➢ If the answer is "no," then ask as a follow up question:

- Do you know whether the remaining inventory was distributed to other companies as well?

A *manufacturer* is the company who creates the product—it is the brand itself. Apple, Hasbro, Nike—these are all brands; therefore, they are manufacturers. Generally, it doesn't make sense for us, the online Amazon sellers, to buy directly from a manufacturer. What you really want to do is ask the manufacturers for their distributors' information—because those distributors will have the cheapest prices. This might seem like an odd proposal, but this is how retail works. Manufacturers allow distributors to buy in larger volumes than they would allow us retailers to buy, and therefore distributors have what's called buying power. You'll almost always get a better deal working with distributors compared to a deal you could make with a manufacturer.

If for some reason you do end up buying from a manufacturer, you should ask:

1. How many retailers buy from you already?

2. Are those retailers brick and mortar stores, or do you sell to online retailers as well?

Remember: Your Suppliers Must Be *Authorized*

We're looking for authorized suppliers only, who sell brand name products. Authorized means that the supplier has the right to sell the product to resellers like you and me. That doesn't mean that your supplier must be working directly with brands, but your supplier does need the full rights to allow you to retail that brand's products. When you buy from an authorized supplier, you will not pay sales tax (assuming you provide your resale certificate). You only avoid paying sales tax when you're buying with the intent to resell or retail. When buying from an unauthorized source, you're expected to use the goods yourself and therefore, you would pay sales tax. Examples of unauthorized ways of getting products are; buying directly from retail stores, clearance stores, garage sales, or Goodwill. For example, you can't buy from Amazon and resell on Amazon, and you can't buy from eBay or Craigslist and resell those items on Amazon either.

You might get away with buying and reselling items from unauthorized sources for a time, but it is **illegal**, and Amazon can suspend you for this behavior, at any time. I don't recommend reselling items from unauthorized sources.

Your Supplier Search

Start searching by making a preliminary list of 10 to 50 potential suppliers to analyze.

In my Online Retail Mastery course, I teach nine, under-the-radar methods for finding suppliers. (This master course has over sixteen hours of videos that walk you through each step of this process and it also contains advanced lessons and other bonuses, including prepared scripts that you can use when talking to your potential suppliers.) This course also explains available business automations.

In this book, however, I will focus on the basic methods for conducting a supplier search, which will provide you with all the information that you need to get started. You can absolutely find your first supplier using the methods described in this next section.

Contacting Brands Directly to ask for their Distributor Information

This is a straightforward approach. Simply get in direct contact with a manufacturer, or you can research a brand online, in order to get information regarding their distributors or wholesalers. The best way to execute this method is explained by the following steps:

1. First, identify a brand. (You can do this by picking brands familiar to you already or by exploring brand names offered at local stores or online.)

2. The manufacturer information is listed on the product's packaging. Many times, the packaging will show the distributor's name as well.

3. Go to the manufacturer's website. (A simple internet search using the brand's name will provide their website information in most cases.)

4. On the brand's website, find a phone number designated as being related to: "B2B," "Retail," "Wholesale Account," or "Trade Account."

5. Call and ask the manufacturer for information regarding how you may buy at wholesale for your retail business or where you could source their products, if not from them directly.

A great example for this last item on this list would be the 1-800-742-7276 phone number for Hasbro. This line is an automated system that gives you instructions for how you might receive information regarding wholesale purchasing. You can leave your email contact and request to receive a list of Hasbro's authorized distributors.

In my Online Retail Mastery course, I provide a list of brands for you to contact directly.

How to Evaluate Suppliers

While you are contacting brands directly (or while exploring any other method of finding suppliers), you're going to come across hundreds of potential suppliers. However, some of these suppliers will not be a good fit for our type of business model. In order to save time, you need to learn how to judge quickly (by evaluating a company's website), whether they are likely to be relevant to our business type. By checking for a few criteria up front, you can avoid wasting countless hours of browsing inconsequential websites and will also avoid wasting time with unproductive phone calls or emails.

If you were to stop to talk to every supplier you find, it would take far too long for you to place your first order. You need to be able to narrow down your potential suppliers list so that you are calling approximately 25 prospective suppliers.

When analyzing your supplier list, you should be investigating the following criteria:

1. Does the supplier sell brand names?

    Most authorized suppliers of brand names will want to advertise that fact. If you see logos or listings on the supplier's website showing big brand names that you recognize—that's a very good sign. Put this supplier on your "call list". If a supplier is using a brand's logo, that means that supplier has been given permission to display the logo, which means they are an authorized seller. (That is, unless that supplier is breaking the law and using the logo without authorization, but most businesses aren't that foolhardy.) Conversely, if you see only generic products on a website, that's a bad sign. Cross this supplier off from your list and move on to begin evaluating the next one.

2. Does the supplier focus mainly on brick and mortar stores?

    Believe it or not, if a supplier's focus is on selling to brick and mortar stores, that's a good thing for you and me. Remember, despite Amazon's massive size, it accounts for only around 5 percent of the retail market. If a supplier works with online sellers only—that's a bad sign, actually. Why would a supplier ignore the majority of the market opportunity? You have to question a supplier's motives for not selling to brick and mortar stores. (There are some exceptions to this rule. I've worked with a couple of good suppliers who focus mainly on Amazon selling because they happened to be comparatively smaller enterprises and more recently established than most other suppliers.)

In general, though, you want to see that a supplier is selling to brick and mortar stores.

3. Does the supplier accept online sellers?

We're looking for suppliers that focus mainly on brick and mortar stores but who are open to working with Amazon FBA sellers like us as well. Otherwise, there is no point in contacting this supplier, right? It may be harder to determine quickly whether the supplier is open to doing business with an online seller, but if their website mentions online sellers, or Amazon, specifically—obviously, that's what we're hoping to find. Suppliers will often note on their websites who they sell products to and that information can usually be found on their Home webpage, or on their About webpage. For example, they may mention that they work with big retail stores, other distributors, online sellers or dropshippers. You won't know for sure until you speak to someone at the company directly, but you should prioritize your potential suppliers call list, by the suppliers that appear to welcome online sellers. If they won't ship directly to Amazon's warehouses, you won't be able to work with them using my strategy.

4. Does the supplier's website look too fancy?

The supplier business is very old-school, so to speak. Most good suppliers are making tons of money already and, frankly, they don't need to focus on whether their websites are flashy looking or whether they have the most high-tech functionality. Needless to say, the suppliers who do not use a website at all, are going to be the hardest kind of supplier to track down, and it stands to follow that this sort of supplier usually doesn't list their product catalog online and doesn't accept online orders either. Furthermore, the best suppliers usually are not optimized for Google. If a supplier is difficult to find and doesn't seem to share much information very readily, that's a good sign.

On the flip side, a fancy looking website may be a bad sign. Good suppliers are busy fulfilling orders. Less useful suppliers may spend more time updating their websites, in an attempt to get new business. A good supplier may have a reasonably decent looking website—but the majority of them will look relatively plain and utilitarian.

Hone your Instincts

When searching for suppliers, you do need to develop the ability to make a judgment call about them—as quickly as possible. Do they meet all the criteria listed above? Yes? Then, put them on your call list. If they don't, move on immediately. There are far too many potentially good suppliers for you to be wasting your time exploring ones that can't possibly fit your needs. Maybe you'll miss out on one or two decent suppliers inadvertently, but remember—all you need is one good supplier to get started. Your most important goal is to find that one, as quickly as possible.

Other Methods

Although I reserve many of my secrets to success lessons for my Online Retail Mastery students, I'm happy to give you a sneak-peek of what that course entails.

Here are some of the topics covered in my Online Retail Mastery course:

- How to find online professional associations for each product category (This is where you will find suppliers.)

- Software that can automate supplier searches for you

- How to browse Google maps to find suppliers

- How to find lists of trade shows and their participants (start with 10times.com)

- How to find the competitors of your existing suppliers

- How to use networking to find suppliers

- How to search forums and databases to find suppliers

Contacting Your Potential Suppliers

Once you have a list of at least ten potential suppliers of brand name products (who may accept Amazon FBA sellers), you will need to set up an account on the online registration system for each supplier. Some suppliers will let you browse their catalog before registering, but they won't let you submit any orders. You might as well register immediately. (It's free and simple to do.)

Typically, you can register directly on the supplier's website. It's usually a mostly intuitive process where you click on **register**, then **sign up** or **application**, and then enter your business information in the online form. The registration link is usually at the top, right-hand side of each website, but sometimes it will be located at the very bottom of the page. Occasionally, a supplier will ask you for "trade references". That means they are looking for a banking institution or some other company that will vouch for you. As a beginner online seller, if you run into this situation, you should probably focus on other suppliers first. The only other hurdle you may encounter is having a supplier ask you for a "Dun & Bradstreet Number". This number is used to identify your company and track its business credit rating. Most suppliers won't require one, but if you find that you need to get a D-U-N-S number, just go to the website, dnb.com and sign up by clicking on the D-U-N-S Number tab near the top of the homepage.

If it's not possible to register online with a supplier, you can locate their contact information on their **Contact** webpage and send an email instead, or, call them directly to ask how you may set up an account.

Personally, I always recommend calling rather than just sending an email.

Make the Call

My secret to ensuring that suppliers respond to me is simple: I make the effort to reach out to them by phone. This principle applies to all contact you have with suppliers—whether it's the initial outreach, or placing an order, or getting payments processed, or researching products or for any other issue you need to resolve. Online sellers who aren't as committed to this business are more apt to just send an email message but will make no further effort than that. Serious sellers will **pick up the phone and make a call.** You want to give the impression that you are serious about your business. Taking the time to make a simple phone call will communicate to another businessperson that you are determined to get things done.

It bears repeating: Retail is old-school. Plan to call the supplier during their business hours. All legitimate suppliers will have at least one person answering incoming calls. If you send a supplier an email and you don't receive a reply, pick up the phone and call them. This is a good example of follow-through. Moreover, putting a voice to your business name will help build a solid, long-term relationship with your suppliers.

Have Your Business Information Readily Available

When registering with suppliers, most will ask for your reseller's permit. If you don't have it on hand, you may end up making an unimpressive first impression on that supplier. Have all your business information ready to go. Be prepared. Some suppliers may ask you for an EIN number as well. The more effort you make to create a legitimate looking business, the better you'll be viewed by suppliers.

Put Yourself in the Supplier's Position

You will make mistakes, and some suppliers will reject you because of it. They might reject you for good reason, or, it may seem to you—for no good reason at all. It is best not to allow yourself to get stressed out over this. All you need is one supplier, and most will be willing to work with you if you're reasonably well prepared.

The inexperienced sellers who end up getting rejected repeatedly are usually the ones who project an entitled attitude. The people who are most likely to fail in this business are those who are disrespectful or rude to suppliers, and who expect preferential treatment but are unwilling to do what is required to earn that kind of privilege. It is important to remember that you're the newcomer in this equation, and the supplier your seeking is the expert with a well-established business. They might want to have your business, but they don't really need it, not as much as you need them, anyway. Suppliers focus more on the long-term aspects of business, rather than on trying to get you to place a one-time order. (You should be focused on long-term connections as well.) Don't expect suppliers to give you their best deals immediately. Building trust takes time. You will have to earn their best deals. Earn those deals by making promises and then delivering on those promises. Make sure to express to your supplier that you intend to build a long-term relationship with them.

Fake It till You Make It

The truth is, as online sellers, we should aim to sell any brand name product that has a high ROI, a quick turnaround and reasonable Buy Box competition. That product may be Hot Wheels, or Clif Bars, Samsung computers or Nautica cologne. It really doesn't matter what it is. That being said, actually telling a supplier that you'll sell anything… may make you sound unprofessional. I recommend finding out which products your supplier focuses on (most specialize in one big category, like video games, or toys or groceries), and then plan to start your conversation with that supplier by asking about a specific product they sell. If you find a video game supplier, tell them you're looking for Xbox and

PlayStation consoles and video games, or that you're looking for Nintendo, or whatever video game product you care to mention. Finding at least one specific relevant product to discuss can make you sound more professional, rather than just saying something like; "I'm an Amazon seller and I just want some products." Also, if you make the effort to talk about a relevant product, your supplier may feel more inclined to look for a deal on that specific type of inventory. When suppliers get the impression that you're a serious buyer, they will be far more motivated to hunt down deals for you.

Suppliers are willing to give you their catalogs or inventory lists, but they often have access to additional products and even better deals as well. By giving them something specific to look for, you've made their job easier. Don't waste a lot of time researching products beforehand. Just pick a popular product that the supplier would likely have. You may wind up ordering something completely different than the product you suggested. That's totally fine. The point is to get the supplier working for you, as soon as possible.

Vetting a Supplier

In order to vet your supplier, you should ask them some specific questions. The first four questions below are simple and straightforward—but if the answer to any of these questions is, "No", then don't waste your time continuing to pursue that supplier.

1. Am I allowed to sell your products online—specifically on Amazon?

    (Some brands have restrictions concerning selling online. Make sure that you confirm that you are allowed to sell their products online.)

    If their products can be sold online, your next question is:

2. Would I be able to use an invoice that I've received from you, to get brand approval from Amazon?

As explained in Chapter 10, some brands and some product categories have special rules and require that you receive approval from Amazon, in order for you to sell them legally. If a supplier has sold these brands on Amazon previously, they'll know the answer to this question, and the supplier should be able to allay any concerns you might have. If the supplier is unable to provide clarification on this matter—that would be a red flag—a bad sign that you will encounter problems when you attempt to sell their product on Amazon.

3. Can you ship directly to Amazon (for FBA sales), and have you shipped to Amazon before?

   If a supplier won't ship to Amazon, that eliminates them from your list. However, it is okay if the supplier hasn't shipped directly to Amazon previously, as long as they're open to shipping to Amazon. You'll need to take extra care when working with a supplier who is shipping to Amazon for the first time to make sure everything goes smoothly with the shipping process. If the supplier has not shipped to Amazon previously, you should be sure to explain the process to them.

4. Are all of your products new?

   Remember, as Amazon sellers we sell **new** products, only. If your products are even slightly used, you'll run into trouble, meaning that Amazon will take down your listing and could even suspend your account as well.

The following questions are optional, but they can help you gather valuable information, as well as, may help you build your relationship with your suppliers.

1. How do you source your inventory? Do you sell closeout items only, or will I be able to reorder inventory?

   Selling closeout products isn't inadvisable, necessarily, because they usually have the highest ROI. However, if a company focuses on closeouts, it does mean that you'll have more work to do overall. You'll have to analyze new products every time your current product sells out and you're forced to order a different type of product.

If the supplier is normal stock (meaning, they can reorder product all the time), your ROI may be lower—but your life will be easier in general. Once you find a profitable product, you can simply continue to reorder it for as long as it remains profitable.

Many suppliers will employ both the closeout and normal stock methods.

2. How often do you get new inventory?

Some suppliers get new inventory every day. For other suppliers, new arrivals happen once a month. It's good to know a supplier's new inventory schedule, that way, you'll know when to check in with that supplier regarding their available products and, obviously, you will know when to place your orders. For example, if a supplier gets new items every month, you can tell them that you plan to buy from them once a month.

3. Do you make most of your sales to brick and mortar retailers, or to online retailers, or to other wholesalers?

Even though there may be no correct answer here, you should be cautious if a supplier says that they mostly sell to Amazon sellers. When that is the case, you'll have to assume that any deal you receive, will also be offered to all of your FBA competitors. If you don't buy all the inventory available for that product—you must assume that your competitors will buy whatever remains. Always err on the side of caution in this situation and, in your profit analysis, account for the fact that this supplier is selling to other Amazon sellers as well. This is especially important when you are starting out in online retail. If you can afford to buy the MOQ only (minimum order quantity), then other sellers will buy the rest of the inventory.

However, if most of a supplier's sales go to brick and mortar stores, it would be relatively more reasonable to assume that the inventory you did not purchase, will not end up with your online retail competitors.

4. Do you have minimum order amounts or minimum order quantities, and, if so, what are they? (Most legitimate suppliers will have a required minimum.)

Sometimes the MOQ refers to the total amount of money you spend per order, and sometimes each item has its own minimum order quantity.

Obviously, you need to make sure you have enough money to meet a supplier's MOQ before proceeding with an order.

5. Are you able to send your current inventory in a CSV file or in some other type of spreadsheet format?

If you use the Crabill Analyzer Software Tool, which can be found at beaucrabill.com, you'll need a spreadsheet with product-identifier numbers (e.g., UPC, EAN or ASIN), and item prices.

Technically, you can do the research on the inventory, manually. However, it would take a very long time to complete the process using that method. Most suppliers will have hundreds of products for you to analyze. There are other kinds of analytic software available as well—but I created my proprietary software out of the frustration I experienced while using the other software that I'd found on the market.

6. What amount of lead time will there be, if I pay for my order today?

Meaning: When will the supplier's products be ready to ship? Ideally, the products will be shipped on the same day that you place your order.

7. What payment types do you accept? Are there any fees involved?

Credit cards usually have a three percent fee added. I often use bank wire transfers to pay for my orders.

And, finally, while the following questions may not be critical in your analysis for choosing your supplier, these questions may help you build a better relationship with your supplier simply by revealing your level of interest:

8. How long have you been in business?

9. Does your company attend trade shows?

If the answer to this trade show question is yes, then ask which trade show they will attend next. You may consider meeting the supplier in person, to further your business relationship with them.

10. Do you have any clients that use Net 30 or Net 60 as a payment method?

Paying Net 30 or Net 60 means that a supplier allows you to pay for your order either 30 days or 60 days, respectively, after you have received your products. Typically, a supplier is not going to offer Net 30 or Net 60 to you until some trust has been established in your business relationship and you have a track record with them.

11. In which product category do you make most of your sales?

12. Where are your warehouses located?

Testing Your Supplier

In order to determine whether your supplier is going to be a good fit for a long-term business relationship, you will have to "test" them, to ensure that you can be confident in their business practices.

There are two ways to test a supplier:

13. Monitor their business activity for a period of 30 to 90 days. (You would do this before placing your first order with them.) If you are not quite ready to place your first order you can instead review a potential supplier's available products, and, choose a few products that you would have an interest in selling. Watch how these products sell on Amazon. Be aware of sales performance and any price fluctuations.

14. This is the surest way to test your supplier to determine whether they will fit your business purposes.

    You don't have to conceal the fact that you are evaluating them. Simply tell the supplier that you're going to watch their business for (whatever number) of days you've decided upon for the evaluation period. I do this with all my vendors. I prefer to invest in a handful of suppliers only, so I need to be selective.

    If everything looks as expected after this investigative period, it's likely that this will be a suitable supplier. If problems arise during this process, move on to evaluate your next supplier option.

15. Evaluate by placing a small order.

Place a small order with the supplier to determine whether the process works out as promised. If the supplier claims that they will ship your products on the same day that you pay for them, do they follow through on this claim? Obviously, conducting this kind of test is somewhat risky. I recommend conducting it only if you are prepared for the possibility that something could go wrong with your first order, meaning, you may lose some money. You may be more comfortable with using the first testing option.

A special note regarding a supplier related problem: Recently, I've seen several online retailers (former Amazon sellers), who have now begun acting and operating as suppliers. They are doing this in order to sell their excess inventory. If their activities and operations are in any way unlawful, then working with these "suppliers" will likely cause trouble for you. This is yet another reason that you want to make sure to follow my supplier evaluation guidelines carefully. You need to make sure the supplier you're using is legitimate.

Be a yardstick of quality. Some people aren't used to an environment where excellence is expected.

— Steve Jobs

Chapter 8

Building Supplier Relationships

The Importance of Building Relationships with Your Suppliers

Building long-term relationships with suppliers is a win-win pursuit. It is crucial for succeeding in online retail. Suppliers want your consistent business, and you want to be rewarded by getting access to their best deals. Working with just one supplier (and, eventually, with a few suppliers), will save invaluable time for you.

When you invest in this business relationship, you'll have a go-to ally in your supplier. Typically, a sales rep (or whomever handles sales inquiries), will be assigned to work with you. As you become more familiar with one another's businesses, they will come to understand what type of products you're looking for, and you can expect that any email that you get from them will likely concern a product you're interested in. This will help your business to become more efficient. And, time is money.

I go over in-depth strategies for building good business relationships in my Online Retail Mastery course. The information in this chapter outlines some tactics from that course.

Treat Your Suppliers Like Humans

This may seem like an obvious thing to do, but many retailers treat suppliers poorly. It is good to remind yourself that your suppliers and sales reps are human beings. They have a job to do. They need to make money too. Remember that there is a human being on the other end of that phone call, text or email. They're not robots. You want to act professional and polite, always, but remember it is important in this industry to be friendly and personable, also. Be sure to treat these new business acquaintances like you would any valued colleague or associate. Making this little bit of extra effort will make you stand out in a sea of mostly inconsiderate clients.

Build Trust

Building trust comes down to making promises and then delivering on them, from the start and in the long run. It's simple, really. (But that doesn't mean it's easy advice to adhere to all of the time.)

Follow these guidelines:

- Don't make false promises.

- Place an order soon after you're finished vetting the supplier.

- Pay for your orders immediately.

- If you need time to analyze their products, tell them that you need time.

- Follow their rules (e.g., adhere to their MOQs).

- Be a benefit to their business.

- Always be prepared.

Think Long Term

As long as you're hitting your target ROI and turnaround time, don't do anything to jeopardize your long-term relationship with a good supplier. You don't want to alienate them by squabbling over pennies. This doesn't mean you have to be a pushover either—it just means to prioritize building a long-term relationship over making a few extra dollars in the short-term.

Be Their Best Client

Conduct yourself like a great client, and your supplier will treat you like a VIP. The reality is that suppliers do pick favorite clients. That may sound biased, but it is a fact of business. Think of ways you can help their business. Explain to them why you buy what you buy. A supplier is going to reserve their best deals for their best clients, and you want to make sure that you're on their short list when they send out emailed offers with those great deals.

To conquer frustration, one must remain intensely focused on the outcome, not the obstacles.

— T.F. Hodge

Chapter 9

Shipping to Amazon

Amazon has numerous FBA locations all over the world and you'll be required to follow their shipping guidelines for each specific product. It is in your best interest to adhere to Amazon's conditions.

Step 1: Determine Whether Amazon Wants Your Products Shipped to Multiple Locations

Before you begin creating any shipping labels, you will need to determine to which locations Amazon wants your products shipped. These location specifics will affect how your supplier breaks down your products for shipment, so, you'll need to provide your supplier with the correct shipping instructions before your order is shipped out, and you should confirm with your supplier that they are willing to follow those instructions. Most suppliers won't mind complying, but it is good business procedure to contact them to confirm that there will be no issues with the shipping requirements.

Step 2: Choose the Type of Packaging

You will need to decide how your supplier should pack your products and make sure to inform your supplier of your preferences. The packing choices are:

1. Individual-packed

2. Case-packed

If every product in a shipment is exactly the same (e.g., 100 pairs of black socks, or 100 black sharpie pens, for instance), you can choose **case-packed**. In this situation, it won't matter whether a bunch of the same items are packed together.

However, if there are **multiple SKUs** (meaning, there are different colors, sizes, quantities, etc.), then you'll need to choose **individually-packed**. For example, you would pick individually-packed if you bought both red Sharpie pens and blue Sharpie pens together, or, you have individual pairs of white socks along with some 3-pack sets of white socks.

Sometimes, Amazon will require different unit quantities be placed into multiple boxes. For example, although you plan to sell the same type of individual pairs of black socks, Amazon may tell you that these like products must be shipped to multiple locations. In that situation, even though the product is all the same, the multiple destinations will require the socks to be shipped in a variety of quantities to these different locations, therefore, you would need to choose **individually-packed**.

Typically, however, the rule for packaging is simple:

When there is **more than one SKU** in a box (or pallet or case), you need to choose **individually-packed**.

When there is **exactly one SKU** per box (or pallet, or case), you can choose **case-packed**.

When you are first starting out, you will choose, individually packed, usually. But when you have the option to choose case-packed, it may save you money. This is because choosing case-packed increases the chances that your items will be sent to **one** FBA warehouse. Amazon won't split up a case.

Step 3: Choose Your Barcode Method

When your products arrive at Amazon's warehouse, Amazon needs to scan either a:

1. Manufacturer barcode, or,

2. An Amazon barcode

Whenever possible, choose the option for Amazon to scan a manufacturer barcode. This will mean that all individual items of the same product (e.g., each one of your 100 packages of Sharpie pens), will use the same barcode. Amazon will allow this for most products. However, for certain products, Amazon will require different, individual barcodes for each item. This means that you'll be forced to choose the option of an Amazon barcode (when entering your product information on Seller Central). If you must label products individually, ask your supplier if they will do this for you. If your supplier declines, then you can simply let Amazon do the labeling at a cost to you of 20 cents per unit.

Amazon typically comingles manufacturer barcodes. Comingling means that, if you and I are both selling Sharpie pens on Amazon, and we both used manufacturer barcodes—Amazon will intentionally combine different sellers' inventories. Basically, Amazon will give each of us the revenue we are due—but in practical terms, for example, they may technically be sending out some of my inventory when you have made a sale, and vice versa. When you look at your Seller Central account, you'll always be able to see how many of your products have been sold and how many are still in the warehouse. Amazon will make sure that this procedure is always done in an equitable way.

There is no downside to using manufacturer barcodes. As always, adhere to Amazon's requirements. Sell real products. Use legitimate suppliers. Sellers who do otherwise will be reprimanded. Amazon is proficient at detecting fake products and will shut down any sellers that break their rules, so don't think that you can get away with selling fake products. Amazon does know which product is yours, specifically, and they will shut down your account if you break their rules.

Always make Amazon happy.

Step 4: Choose Your Method of Delivery

There are two ways to send your products from your supplier to an Amazon FBA warehouse. If Amazon tells you to send your product to multiple locations, be sure to analyze your shipments separately.

Delivery Types

(SPD) Small Parcel Delivery

SPD refers to a typical FedEx or UPS shipment in a small truck.

You'll ship via SPD for smaller shipments. To ship SPD, your shipment must meet these criteria:

- There must be less than 150 pounds total being sent to this one location.

- No boxes over 50 pounds

- No boxes larger than 25 inches on any side (height, length or width)

When you choose SPD, you'll have three shipping company options: UPS, FedEx or, "Other." UPS and FedEx are Amazon Preferred shipping companies—meaning that by choosing one of those two companies, you will get big discounts. Unless you're shipping internationally, UPS or FedEx will likely be your cheapest shipping option. FedEx is often cheapest, by a few cents. UPS is usually fastest, therefore, most suppliers use UPS. If you want to save a few cents, you can ask your supplier to ship using

FedEx, but my position is that UPS should be your default shipping option. Occasionally, when your supplier simply will not use UPS, they will tell you to choose a different shipping company.

LTL (Less Than Load/Truckload)

If your shipment doesn't meet the SPD criteria, you'll need to use an LTL shipment. This means that a freight truck will load your items amongst shipments belonging to other individuals. All the items are separated by pallets, instead of by individual boxes. Your items will be packed into either large boxes, or cases—and then shrink-wrapped onto a pallet.

Standard pallet dimensions are 48 inches by 40 inches. Amazon has its own restrictions concerning pallet dimensions and will not accept items measuring over 72 inches tall. You may need to ask your supplier to break up your items, if a shipment is going to exceed Amazon's maximum allowable dimensions. As a beginner, it's not likely that you'll have to address this issue, but you should make note of this Amazon shipping requirement.

Sending LTL shipments mean more moving parts because it requires that you deal with a freight company. Here are some tips that will ensure that you get the cheapest rates, fastest shipping and proper execution:

- Be sure to forward your Bill of Lading (BOL) to your supplier.

- The BOL is a signed document confirming that the freight company picked up your pallet (shipment). You'll need your supplier to sign the BOL, as they will do the actual shipping to Amazon. However, Amazon emails the BOL to *you*. You must remember to forward the BOL to your supplier. (Your supplier will know what to do with it.) You won't need to sign the BOL. Simply forward the BOL email to your supplier.

- A BOL is usually valid for approximately 24 to 48 hours.

When filling out details for an LTL shipment, Amazon gives you three options for uploading information regarding dimensions and weight. Those options are:

1. Web Form

2. Upload File

3. Skip Box Information (and apply manual fee)

Always choose *Web Form*.

Choose a Freight Class

> Simply, the larger the freight class, the higher the cost. The most expensive freight class costs $500, and the lowest priced class costs $50. Obviously, you'll want to choose the least expensive option that will work for the size of your shipment.

Pallets must be labeled. However, a label is not required for an individual box or case. If your supplier is willing to apply a label to a box or case, that's great, but if the supplier doesn't do it, Amazon will wind up doing it for you. Amazon may not divulge this fact voluntarily, because it creates a little extra work for them—but they will do it. The reason Amazon does this is because all pallets are shrink-wrapped, and, Amazon sends all pallets to their pallet-LTL team, which removes the shrink wrap in order to take out all the boxes the pallet contains.

Box and case labels are not mandatory when shipping using LTL, but you'll receive both pallet labels and case labels via email. Send both label types via email to your supplier but let your supplier know that they're not required to use the case labels. Amazon will provide you with the estimated pick-up date and time and will let you know which freight company will handle the pick-up. I prefer to relay all this information to my supplier.

Additional Important Shipping Tips

Choosing the Number of Shipping Boxes

> Whenever possible, you should choose the option, "everything in one box". This is the least expensive option.

Entering Your Supplier's Contact Information

> When you are creating a shipment on Amazon, on the final page of the process you will see that Amazon uses your contact information for the shipping details. You need to **change this information** so that it lists your supplier's contact information instead. By default, Amazon will use your contact information on forms, but that means that Amazon would contact you, rather than your supplier, should any problems arise with the shipment. Needless to say, you wouldn't be able to assist Amazon with any shipping issues, so it is very important that you make sure that Amazon has the correct contact information for your supplier. Simply change the contact information to show your supplier's phone number, address and email. Amazon will still send the BOL and all tracking information to you. Your supplier is likely to receive the BOL from Amazon via email as well, however, you should forward to your supplier the BOL that you receive from Amazon—just to ensure that your supplier sees a copy of the BOL.

Confirmation

> Double-check that you've entered all details accurately and then click on **calculate**. After you have confirmed that the total cost that appears is similar to what you calculat-

ed, click on **accept charges**. You will receive your shipping labels via email as a PDF file. Make sure to forward these labels to your supplier.

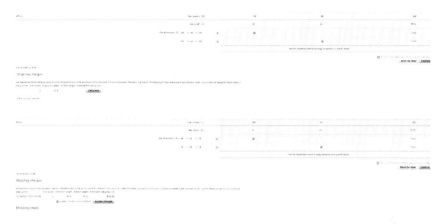

Congratulations! When you've reached this point, you'll be (essentially) done with your online retail sales order. However, my recommendation is that it is good business practice to continue to keep tabs on your orders, even though Amazon and your supplier will be handling the bulk of the logistics from this point on.

Other Possible Shipping Scenarios

The following examples are special case scenarios related to shipping:

Hazmat Material

It is possible that you may end up selling products that are considered "hazmat", which, in this case, refers to items that are defined by Amazon as potentially hazardous materials. This product type has its own set of special rules and it isn't always eligible to be sent to FBA warehouses. Sometimes this may include something as commonplace as items that contain batteries. Also, Amazon will allow certain sellers to sell hazmat products, but won't give other sellers the same privilege. In order to get approval, you will need to contact Amazon. Amazon will require that you provide paperwork to prove that you're selling new products from legitimate sources, only. Most sellers won't bother to participate in this product segment—so that means that there's less competition in this category. However, as mentioned, not all hazmat products are eligible for FBA. A seller may be required to sell the hazmat product using FBM. The specifics of selling FBM (Fulfilled by Merchant) are discussed briefly in this book in Chapter 11, however, I give in-depth instruction in my Online Retail Mastery course regarding how to sell using FBM.

Buying Individual Items but Selling Multi-Packs

Sometimes, you may find that an item that your supplier is selling to you in an individual quantity is being sold on Amazon in multipacks. For example, your supplier sells individual Colgate toothbrushes to you—but that same type of toothbrush is being sold in packs of three on Amazon.

To resolve this sort of quantity discrepancy, you need to make sure that you buy the correct number of total units from your supplier. For example, if you want to sell 100 packs of three, you should buy 300 individual units from your supplier.

When entering your product information on Amazon, however, you would enter, "100 units". You will then receive labels for 100 units. Generally, suppliers label things in individual units. But Amazon labels items however they are going to be sold. For example, something containing a pack of 10 items, may be treated as one unit, as far as Amazon is concerned.

Ideally, though, you'll do one of two things:

1. Have your supplier write the specifics on the boxes (e.g., "sold as a pack of three").

2. Have your supplier bundle the products (e.g., put a rubber band or shrink-wrap around three items to create a "three pack". Most suppliers are familiar with bundling.

How to Prepare Special Products

For the most part, U.S. suppliers prepare products as needed, without requiring any involvement from you. However, in some rare cases, Amazon may tell you that a product requires additional special preparations such as, an item needs bubble-wrapping. Should one of these rare occasions arise, you can check with your supplier first, to see if they are willing to take care of this special packing prep. If the supplier declines, you will need to select the option (in the **Manage Shipments** section on Amazon's site), that allows Amazon to prep your products for a small fee.

It is also a good idea to get in the habit of double-checking that your supplier has remembered to seal all liquids and protects all glass or breakable items.

If you don't do it, nothing's possible.

— Jack Ma

Chapter 10

Getting Ungated

Ungating

I cover ungating in-depth in my Online Retail Mastery course, but in this chapter, I will provide a general explanation of the process concerning getting ungated with Amazon.

Ungating is simply the process of getting approved to sell products that are, for one reason or another, restricted by Amazon. These restrictions exist to protect sellers who do things properly, and to penalize sellers who fail to follow Amazon's rules. Amazon's chief concern is that you work with authorized suppliers only. The fact is that the average Amazon seller won't take the time to go through the process of getting ungated. However, getting ungated is not difficult, usually, and by making a little effort to get ungated, you'll be allowed to sell products that have less competition in their category. Ungated products don't have less demand, but they do have less supply. This scenario means an opportunity for you to achieve greater profits.

There are three types of ungating (meaning also, three types of Amazon restrictions). Those three types are: main categories, sub-categories and brands. The way to find out whether you're gated (restricted) for a certain product is by going to the **Seller Central** webpage, and then clicking on the option to **add a product**. Enter the product type in question. If a **sell yours** button appears, you're good to go. This means that you have no restrictions for selling this product.

However, if, instead, you see a message that reads, **request approval**, then you'll need to get ungated for that category, subcategory or brand. Sometimes, getting ungated is as simple as answering a few questions. Other times, getting ungated can be a more involved process. The process required is all dependent upon the product. The rules regarding ungating change regularly, as well. Categories like beauty and grocery tend to be more difficult to undertake. Getting ungated for these specific categories rarely happens automatically. However, once you have established an account with consistent sales and a good track record, you will find that you will be able to get ungated in almost anything. There's no official figure, but by my estimation, once you achieve around $50,000 in sales per month, you should not encounter any issues related to restrictions.

Even as a beginner, you can get ungated in many categories. Simply follow the instructions described later in this chapter which take you through each step that is required to become ungated.

I recommend getting ungated in all the easy categories as soon as possible. For example, at this time, clothing, luggage and travel are among the easiest categories—but, you can review all Amazon's restrictions online at: https://sellercentral.amazon.com/gp/help/external/G200333160.

In general, it is more difficult to get ungated for subcategories. Remember, however—getting ungated will allow you to sell restricted products in which you'll have less competition from other sellers than you would otherwise. For example, for dietary supplements, you usually need to provide an FDA (Food and Drug Administration) legal document. You can ask your supplier if they have the necessary legal document for this type of product.

In comparison to subcategories, getting ungated for brands is easy, as long as you're working with authorized suppliers.

During the ungating process, you can expect that Amazon will ask for one of the two following items:

1. A letter from the manufacturer, or

2. An invoice from your supplier

Typically, you'll send an invoice to Amazon from your authorized supplier—except in the rare instance that you've bought directly from a brand. In that case, an invoice must be a finalized invoice (meaning you've already paid for the products). Always pay for your product before asking your supplier to help you get ungated. Also, make sure that all your business information is accurate on the invoice, and that you use the supplier's contact information. Amazon will contact them and, assuming all is in order, you will get ungated soon thereafter. This process may take ten minutes or may take up to as long as an hour to complete.

Additional Ungating Tip

When submitting an invoice, include all the following information in the "comments" section of the submission form:

• the number of units

• the name of the items

• the date you purchased the items

• the name of the supplier

• Doing this will help Amazon's algorithm and may work to get you approved quicker.

If your supplier's invoice is declined by Amazon, first check for any minor errors that may have been made while entering information into the submission form. Misspelling your business name or mistyping your supplier's phone number could be enough to get you denied, temporarily.

If you verify that you did not make any errors, there could be two possible reasons for the denial:

- Your supplier hasn't gone through the approval process on Amazon yet. (If this is the cause, you will need to ask the supplier to complete the process).

- Your supplier is being dishonest with you. (They're not admitting to you that they're not an authorized supplier.)

- It is not good news to find out that your supplier is not an authorized supplier. If this occurs, you should stop working with them immediately and you should try to get a refund.

Finally, if you find that you are not able to do the ungating process yourself, you can use an ungating service. As part of my Online Retail Mastery course, I share the names of companies which can help you get ungated. Using this service, my students have gotten ungated in even the toughest categories (such as beauty and topicals), and, in some cases, students were able to get ungated before they had made a single sale on Amazon.

You don't have to be great to start, but you have to start to be great.

— Zig Ziglar

Chapter 11

Winning the Buy Box

Understanding the Buy Box

When selling on Amazon, you can fulfill your inventory through FBA (Fulfilled by Amazon), or FBM (Fulfilled by Merchant). FBA allows you to use Amazon's fulfillment center resources, meaning Amazon's employees handle your merchandise logistics for you, and your items are stored in Amazon's warehouses. FBA sellers always have an advantage over FBM sellers with regard to the Buy Box. Most of my sales are made FBA whereas only about five percent of my sales are made via FBM. There are some products where it is more profitable to use FBM due to certain shipping fees that Amazon charges in some FBA scenarios. Although I discuss FBM in greater detail in my online course, I will explain it briefly in this book, as most sales will be conducted using FBA instead.

Winning the Buy Box Using FBM (Fulfilled by Merchant)

Winning the Buy Box as an FBM seller is a much more complicated approach when compared with using FBA to win the Buy Box. You will need to do the following in order to win the Buy Box using FBM:

1. *Price* your item 15.1 percent lower than the lowest FBA seller's price.

2. *Choose a fast shipping method.* The faster the promised

delivery time, the better the odds that you will win the Buy Box as an FBM seller.

3. *Have positive Seller Reviews*: On Amazon, there are Product Reviews and there are Seller Reviews. Customers are given the chance to leave a Seller Review concerning the buying experience they had with you. The higher the percentage of positive reviews that you have—along with the greater number of positive reviews you accrue—the better the odds are that you will win the Buy Box as an FBM seller. Having even one positive review is very beneficial. Of course, there is a significant difference between having just one positive review compared to having thousands of positive reviews, however, it is really critical that you have at least one positive review, as compared to having none at all.

4. *Establish a sales history*. If you are new to Amazon, make sure to sell **FBA** initially. Accumulate some seller reviews. My recommendation would be to sell FBA for six months before attempting to sell FBM. If you attempt to sell FBM any sooner than that, you will most likely find it challenging to get sales.

Notice in the image that follows that there are no FBA sellers for this product. This is an example of an FBM seller. This scenario may result from a variety of causes but, usually, the reason no FBA sellers exist is simply due to the fact that these sellers on this listing are not knowledgeable of the best ways to utilize Amazon. Another possible issue could be that the product is classified as a hazmat item, meaning it is considered too dangerous to stock in Amazon's warehouse, and Amazon refuses to sell it FBA.

The arrows in the following example point to: Ships from and sold by Photo Background.

Photo Background, is the name of the third-party seller who is selling via FBM.

Winning the Buy Box using FBA

Winning the Buy Box using FBA is a much more straightfoward method compared to using FBM. The reason this approach is simpler is because your seller reviews, your shipping time and your sales history **do not matter**. None of those factors are applicable. Your seller reviews are irrelevant because Amazon is fulfilling the orders. So, whether or not you are considered a "good" seller doesn't matter, because Amazon is going to handle everything related to the logicstics of this product. Furthermore, the item will be shipped via FBA so your shipping isn't a factor. Lastly, as sales history doesn't come into play either, someone (like me) who has been selling for several years will have no advantage over you, a newer, less experienced seller.

It is important to remember that when selling FBA, your product must be in new condition and you should match the current Buy Box price if there are other FBA sellers winning the Buy Box already.

This image below shows a University of Alabama Crimson Tide slipper, where an FBA seller is winning the Buy Box. The arrows point to: Sold by Happy Feet and Comfy Feet, and, Fulfilled by Amazon. The seller is Happy Feet and Comfy Feet and they are selling this product using FBA.

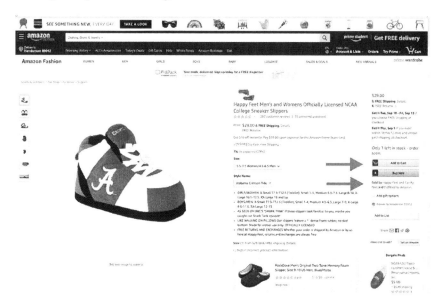

Over half of all Amazon's customers are Prime members and many non-members buy from listings with the "Prime" logo anyway—because, those listings are fulfilled by Amazon. The Prime logo signals reliability. Amazon rewards sellers who satisfy their customers' preferences. Amazon does this by guaranteeing equal Buy Box rotation for all sellers of new, FBA products, sold at the market price. When a shopper clicks on a listing, Amazon's algorithm will choose from amongst all buy-box-eligible sellers and will display one of those as the Buy Box.

Amazon on the Buy Box

Regarding the product seen in the following image, Amazon is actually the seller of this item.

In 2017, 48 percent of the product sales on Amazon were sold by Amazon itself. In 2018, these sales equaled 42 percent. In a year-end letter to his employees, Jeff Bezos remarked, "Third-party sales have grown from 3 percent of total sales to a total of 58 percent currently. To put it bluntly, third-party sellers are kicking our first-party butt."

The numbers are trending up for third-party sales, however, the Buy Box rules are still a little different when Amazon itself is the one selling the product.

When Amazon is on the Buy Box, the only way for you to win the Buy Box is by setting your price lower than the price Amazon has set.

Furthermore, if Amazon then matches your lower price, Amazon will win the Buy Box anyway.

You can check graphs in Keepa to see whether Amazon has matched other sellers' prices. Looking at the Keepa graph below, notice that Amazon was on the listing for a short period of time. The dotted line representing the Buy Box price is lower than the top edge of the highlighted section. (This highlighted area represents Amazon.) In this scenario, it would be okay for you to sell this product. You will be able to sell your item at a lower price than Amazon's price.

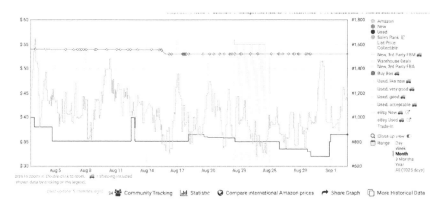

In the following graph the image shows an example of when to steer clear of a sale! Whenever the dotted line is adjacent to the highlighted area, you should skip this product and move on to the next one.

No Buy Box

The final scenario we need to explore regarding winning the Buy Box is the occasion where there is no Buy Box available.

The following image is an example of this sort of circumstance:

This PS4 product has no Buy Box.

The listing has a purchasing button that reads, See All Buying Options.

In a sense, Amazon is penalizing this product listing by making the Buy Box unavailable.

Amazon will do this on an item which carries a price that Amazon's algorithm believes has been set too high for its customers. This product is a video game. All video games have an MSRP (manufacturer's suggested retail price) of $59.99, except for special edition games. I know this to be true because, for one thing, I grew up playing video games, but also, because I now sell millions of dollars of video games.

Therefore, when any video game is set at a price above $59.99, Amazon will ding that item, so to speak, and will not provide a Buy Box for its listing.

With no Buy Box available, the customer is forced to take a few extra steps to complete the sale. This can result in the loss of sales if the customer becomes disinterested.

Of the customers that continue to pursue the item by clicking on the, See All Buying Options button, most will seek to buy the item from the FBA seller with the cheapest price available. If multiple FBA sellers exist with the same product price, then the customer will likely narrow those available options by examining the seller reviews.

My favorite things in life don't cost any money. It's really clear that the most precious resource we all have is time.

— Steve Jobs

Chapter 12

Simplify Your Process with Software

In the online retail business, just like in most other enterprises, time is an important factor. If you wait a week to tell a supplier that you want in on a deal or offer, the opportunity will probably be gone. If you buy too much inventory, you could miss out on other opportunities because of the extended amount of time it will take to sell the surplus products you have already.

In online retail, the faster you are able to source products the more money you stand to make.

Four years ago, my usual way of analyzing products was done by scanning through large spreadsheet lists of inventory. Typically, these spreadsheets would contain lists consisting of well over 1,000 products.

I am able to discern, within about 20 seconds, whether a product is a good investment, or not. For the average person, this product evaluation process may take anywhere from just a few minutes to as long as ten minutes.

Consider this equation based on my processing speed: 1000 products x 20 seconds of evaluation per product = over 5 ½ hours of time invested.

Even at my accelerated pace, I was still using up the equivalent of more than half of a business day to evaluate product.

Still, back then, it was worth my time. I would find thousands of dollars in profit by analyzing a spreadsheet this way.

On a modest day, let's say I realized $800 profit from my product selection. That profit, divided by the more than 5 hours of my time that had been spent to find it, still equaled a considerable wage, earning me about $145 per hour.

Then I discovered virtual assistants. Virtual assistants are outsourced employees who are educated, highly trained workers with computer skills. In my experience of hiring them, they were frequently based in the Philippines. The cost to hire this type of virtual assistant is about $4 per hour, due to the comparatively low cost of living in their country combined with the value of the U.S. dollar compared to their currency. Everyone I hired was fluent in English as well, so, I started teaching them to do the time-consuming inventory analysis process for me. Now, instead of spending over five hours doing the work all by myself, I was able to employ multiple virtual assistants to do much of the work for me.

I still use virtual assistants today, but where simplifying my product analysis process was concerned, I ended up discovering something even more effective.

A friend recommended an analytical software program where I was able to upload the inventory spreadsheets that I received and within only an hour of time, I was able to discern which of the available products would be winners.

Initially, I was very glad that my friend turned me on to this analytical software, however, I soon realized that the program had numerous functionality issues. To start, I had to buy a Windows-based PC in order to be able to use the software because it would not run on an Apple Mac OS. Also, the program could not handle large file uploads—it had issues processing the data correctly.

After using the program (and struggling with it), for a few months, I decided the best solution to the problem was to just make my own analytic software.

So that's what I did.

It took seven months of hard work to develop my program (with two of those months spent putting the program through its paces and beta testing my design). Add in a fair amount of stress, and a lot of my own money, and... my software program was created! The software program itself took only three months to develop, but I spent an additional four months perfecting it before I was willing to release it for public use.

Within 48 hours of introducing my proprietary program, the Crabill Analyzer Software Tool gained over 500 subscribers.

As with the production and release of this book, and for that matter, with any project I'm involved in, I refuse to launch a product until I am sure that the quality is top notch and I feel confident that it will be the best offer on the market. When I reached the point that I felt my software product was the best tool available, I launched it. I use the software every day. There is absolutely no way that I would have been able to grow my business to its current level of success, without the benefit of having this analytical tool.

A key factor in the successful functionality of the Crabill Analyzer Software Tool is that it was built and perfected by me—an actual Amazon seller—along with the expertise and input of professional software engineers. My vast experience with selling on Amazon gave me an insightful perspective which was a critical factor in determining exactly what this analytical software required in order to function properly for this type of business.

Here is how the software works:

Step 1. Access Inventory. Get access to a supplier's product list in a spreadsheet format.

Note: In my Online Retail Mastery course pictured in the following screenshot, I offer nine proven methods for finding suppliers.

Step 2. Download the inventory spreadsheet onto your computer, as a CSV file.

Then, login to the software program. (You will need to go online to beaucrabill.com to purchase The Crabill Analyzer Software Tool, in order to proceed with the following steps.)

Step 3. **Upload** the inventory spreadsheet into the software platform.

Analyzer Tool

Please upload the CSV here. Download example here.

File   [Choose File] cosemetics - Sheet1.csv

Step 4. Process the spreadsheet information. Before processing the spreadsheet, make sure that the product identity codes match up. A product identity code is a unique identifier for a specific product. Product identity codes in the Amazon world appear in the forms of ASINs, UPCs, EANs, or ISBNs. ASIN stands for Amazon Standard Inventory Number. It is a listing identifier that is unique to your product on Amazon. UPC stands for Universal Product Code. Typically, suppliers will use a UPC to identify a product as the UPC code is more universally known. EAN stands for European Article Number. If you are working with European suppliers, they will use a EAN instead of a UPC. An ISBN is an International Standard Book Number, a unique code used to identify a book.

The analyzing software tool will work only when it is aware of which specific product type your supplier has. The tool can read ASINs, UPCs, or EANs. If your supplier is using ASINs, for example, make sure to tell the software that the product identifier is an ASIN.

Next, set up the **Price** column. The software program needs to know what your product purchase costs will be in order to determine profits. Make sure that whatever appears in the price column on the spreadsheet you are analyzing, matches precisely to the data you enter into the price field in the software.

Once you've input the price information, you are ready to process.

Analyzer Tool

Identify products by:	ASIN ⊙ UPC EAN
UPC field:	UPC
Price field	PRICE
My purchase costs are:	Per item
E-mail me when the processing is complete:	☑

PROCESS

Step 5: Filter. Using the data you have for every single product on the spreadsheet that you've just processed, you will now apply filters, in order to find the most profitable products. In my opinion, this is where the fun begins. It takes just five to ten minutes to process a spreadsheet containing 1000 products.

≥ Sales Rank   ≤ Sales Rank

≥ Profit   ≤ Profit

≥ ROI   ≤ ROI

search   reset

∧∨ ASIN	∧∨ UPC	∧∨ Purchase Cost	∧∨ EAN	∧∨ Title	∧∨ Sales Rank	∧∨ Buy Box or lowest price	∧∨ Total cost	∧∨ Profit	∧∨ ROI	Link
B00ES9D7HG	045496891503	9.00		Nintendo 3DS Compatible with 3DS / 3DS XL / 2DS AC Adapter	118.00	8.99	15.34	-6.35	-71.00	https://www.amazno.co
B00S8H7AJO	722674700382	17.00		Ace Combat Assault Horizon Legacy+ - Nintendo 3DS	26085.00	29.50	25.64	3.86	23.00	https://www.amazon.co
B00CMD7BL2	879278006126	15.00		Adventure Time: Explore the Dungeon Because I DON'T KNOW! 3DS	15346.00	16.00	21.61	-5.61	-37.00	https://www.amazon.co
B0081K5TV8	879276380082	15.00		Adventure Time: Hey Ice King! Why'd you steal our garbage?!! - Nintendo 3DS	10812.00	19.23	22.09	-2.86	-19.00	https://www.amazon.co

In this business, not every product deal offered will be a profitable one. Around five percent of the deals I analyze end up being good deals. Reviewing the previous screenshot, three products are unfavorable and there is only one product that has a positive ROI. (Not visible in this screenshot are an additional 207 products that appear on the entire spreadsheet.)

To find the best product deals, my software allows you to filter the results so that ONLY the favorable deals appear.

This is achieved by applying three filters.

Filter 1: Sales Rank. The lower the product's sales rank number is, the faster a product is selling. A sales ranking of "1", would mean that the product is flying off the shelves, so to speak. In my online course I provide guidelines regarding what sales ranks to adhere to, based on the product type. In the video game category, for example, I set the maximum Sales Rank to 15,000. Specifically, that means that for this filter, I would set the Sales Rank filter at greater than or equal to 1, and less than or equal to 15,000.

≥ Sales Rank	≤ Sales Rank	
≥ Profit	≤ Profit	
≥ ROI	≤ ROI	

search   reset

Filter 2: Profit. For this filter type, I use a range of greater than or equal to $1.00 and less than or equal to $3,000.

The reason for setting some sort of maximum regarding profit, is that it is possible that a supplier may omit pricing for an item. This could occur if a supplier simply makes an error while inputting product data. If a supplier forgets to price an item, and, you don't have a limit set for the profit filter, a product may populate through the filter and may be displayed as a potential buy candidate, when it really shouldn't be considered a good deal. You can choose whatever upper limit you prefer. By setting a maximum, you eliminate unpriced items.

Filter 3: ROI. I set this filter range at greater than or equal to 5% and less than or equal to 3000%.

The reason for setting the lower range to include deals that have an ROI as low as 5 percent is that there is always the possibility that I will be able to negotiate with my suppliers on price. If by negotiating, I'm able to knock off a few dollars from the price per unit, then the ROI for this deal could increase to over 10 percent, which would make it a viable investment. I do not invest in products with a ROI lower than 10 percent.

The following screenshot shows how these settings appear in the software for the three filter ranges I've just described.

≥	1		≤	15000
≥	1	⌄	≤	3000
≥	5		≤	3000

search | reset

After you click on the search button, the settings you've chosen will filter the results so that only profitable product deals populate.

Step 6. Double check your analysis and then make your order.

Originally, 207 products were listed on this specific spreadsheet.

Now, as shown on the following graphic, the software filters have narrowed down the selection so that the nine potentially profitable deals are displayed.

∧ ∨ ASIN	∧ ∨ UPC	∧ ∨ Purchase Cost	∧ ∨ EAN	∧ ∨ Title	∧ ∨ Sales Rank	∧ ∨ Buy Box or lowest price	∧ ∨ To
B01IW7Z6BA	045496744090	16.00		Nintendo Selects: Lego City Undercover: The Chase Begins - Nintendo 3DS	6283.00	24.99	23.96
B071JQRWJ7	730865300266	24.00		Radiant Historia: Perfect Chronology - Nintendo 3DS	2669.00	34.91	33.45
B002IOGKA4	013388305018	22.00		Resident Evil: The Mercenaries 3D	13015.00	32.91	31.15
B005OSVLI2	013388305087	22.00		Resident Evil: Revelations	13703.00	33.26	31.20
B008J16AQK	047875767294	24.00		Angry Birds Trilogy Nintendo 3DS	6925.00	35.70	33.57
B007BGUGVO	045496741983	25.00		Mario Tennis Open	5482.00	38.40	34.97
B004XV9F62	010086611069	33.00		Mario & Sonic at the London 2012 Olympic Games, Nintendo 3DS	14590.00	49.99	44.71
B011806LG2	047875770645	17.00		Teenage Mutant Ninja Turtles Master Splinter's Training Pack - Nintendo 3DS	5065.00	31.38	25.92
B01HFRICLE	719593140115	22.00		River City: Tokyo Rumble with FREE Limited Edition Kunio Keychain	5091.00	99.98	41.21

The Crabill Analyzer Software Tool is fully accurate with regard to analyzing product inventory. However, make sure that you complete the follow up work to this automated product inventory analysis by checking out competitors, and reviewing the Keepa graphs, before calling your supplier to place an order. The Crabill Analyzing Software tool helps simplify these final steps by providing a clickable link that connects directly to the related Amazon webpage.

Bonus Step: Filter for most profitable or fastest selling.

If you are like me and you're trying to find the most amount of inventory that is profitable, then I would suggest clicking on the up arrow found on the Sales Rank filter form. This action will show you the products that sell the most on Amazon.

If you are just getting started in your online sales business, I would search for the products with the most amount of profit or ROI. Typically, you will be able to find deals that have very high ROIs. For example, on the following spreadsheet screenshot, there is a product that has a 267 percent ROI.

This product has a sales rank of 5,091. That ranking is acceptable in the video game category, but it does mean that it is not flying off the shelves. However, it is selling close to 100 times per month. This example represents a great product for a beginner Amazon seller. If you achieved 100 sales per month, and have invested in

100 units at $22.00 each, that means that you could realize $5,800 in profit on a $2,200 investment. In my opinion, turning $2,200 into $8,000, in one month… makes for a good month.

Fail fast.

— Phil Knight

Chapter 13

Tough Lessons

During my many years of selling online, I've made a few missteps and encountered some unfortunate experiences as well. As I mentioned earlier in this book, I did not have the advantage of having an experienced mentor to "show me the ropes," in all the aspects of online selling nor did I have any sort of guidebook that I could reference to help me navigate through the learning curve of selling on Amazon. I created this book to help you avoid unfortunate pitfalls, like falling prey to scams, and to prevent you from experiencing some of the downsides I've encountered in selling online.

In sharing with you some of the errors that I made and problems I've experienced, I hope I will be able to help you steer clear of making these sorts of avoidable mistakes in your own ventures in selling online. Avoiding mistakes will help save both your valuable time... and your money.

Air Compressors

At the time that I first decided to add selling on Amazon to my other business enterprises, I also made my first sizeable financial investment for a product purchase.

In relative terms, the invested amount wouldn't seem so large to me today, but at the time, the amount of money I was investing, $15,000, was a serious chunk of change for me.

I had decided to purchase $15,000 worth of ASOTV air compressors from a supplier, who happened to be a new distributor to me.

I had calculated that I would make 35 percent on my investment and that I would sell out of the compressors within 30 days. I made my order and sent the shipment of air compressors on two pallets to Amazon.

When the products arrived, they started selling very fast, over the first couple of days, at least.

Suddenly, however, I got a notification from Amazon telling me that they had removed my listing for the air compressors.

I was stunned. Stunned and panicked. I had no idea why Amazon had removed my listing.

When I checked my Amazon account for details, I saw that the manufacturer had stated that I was not permitted to sell their products.

I called my supplier immediately.

Long story short, my supplier was aware that I wasn't going to be allowed to sell this product on Amazon but, they sold the product to me anyway. Evidently, this particular brand of compressor, Telebrands, is one of the few manufacturers on Amazon that does not want its products to be sold by other sellers. Any outside seller attempting to sell their product, will have his or her listing taken down. The lesson here, besides the obvious lesson that you should not attempt to sell Telebrand products on Amazon, is that you need to make sure to confirm with your supplier that you will be permitted to resell their product on Amazon. I go over this matter in some detail in the chapters that concern supplier relationships and finding suppliers. As I mentioned before, I did not have the benefit of any mentor, or manual, to guide me through these specific kinds of potential hazards regarding selling on Amazon. I hope, by sharing my own unfortunate experiences, you will be able to avoid going through them in your own business deals.

Chasing the Quick Buck May Forfeit your Future Fortune

The series of events revealed in the following story describe an incident that really bothered me.

There are individuals who lack the proper work ethic, commitment and patience that are all necessary traits for building a solid financial foundation by honest means. These people look to take short cuts instead and are really just looking to make a quick dollar, regardless of how that is achieved, and irrespective of whether they might be conning someone else in the process.

This situation involved a few people who did not use good judgment, were not acting ethically and who were intent only on making some quick cash in the short term, regardless of the long-term consequences of their actions.

Of the people who become interested in the system that I teach and the business opportunities I present, most are committed to learning how to conduct their business the right way, and most are focused on creating a financially successful business that will be viable for the long haul.

However, there are people who look to take advantage of others by whatever means possible. We all see different types of scam offers pop up online, which then disappear before very long, only to resurface in a slightly different form sometime later.

In our current fast-paced digital world, information is spread quickly, and, for the most part, unethical businesses and people are exposed fairly fast and are shut down—at least for a while.

A case involving deceptive sales practices, that I ended up having to confront personally, revolved around a business created by a person named Parker who had actually bought my online course. He achieved great results using my program. After just a few months, he was transacting sales of over a $1,000 per day. In fact, this student reached out to my support team to say that he would love to work for me. He also expressed a desire to be a moderator in my Facebook group. He was a "rock star" student overall and, reportedly, one of my biggest fans.

But then... I found out that he had started up a wholesale company.

My first reaction to hearing this news was one of skepticism. I cautioned him to be careful in proceeding with this plan because he hadn't been in this business for very long yet. For that reason, I was sure that he hadn't yet established the crucial business connections that are needed to start a successful wholesale enterprise. Parker and his business partner explained to me that they had discovered the good business connections that they needed. Upon hearing that, I just decided to let the situation be, and did not say anything further on the matter, with the exception that I did ask Parker and his partner not to promote their wholesale business to my groups.

However, a month later, I began receiving emails at support@beaucrabill.com asking whether I'd heard of a company named _____. [I will refer to that company here only as: "XYZ" even though that is not the actual name of the company involved in this incident.] This company was owned by Parker.

Now, it is not unusual for me to get emails from clients asking whether I'm familiar with one supplier or another. And, it is not uncommon that my response to these inquiries would be that even if I haven't heard of a particular company, it doesn't mean that there is something wrong with that supplier. Some of my best students work with suppliers I've never heard of before. In general, any supplier in the USA is, most likely, okay to work with. I'm not talking about whether they'll be profitable for you; that is a separate issue. I'm referring to American suppliers' legitimacy in general. The point I'm emphasizing here is that it is illegal to sell counterfeit products in the USA, and it is unlawful to misappropriate people's money. So, it follows that, as a reseller, you don't have to worry about getting scammed—for the most part, anyway—because most businesspeople won't want to risk getting into legal trouble themselves.

In this scenario, however, after another month passed, I noticed that three more emails were sent to our support team regarding sellers who had had their accounts suspended for selling Play-Station controllers. Amazon had stated that the controllers were counterfeit.

This struck me as odd. Using the business model that I teach; it is not typical that a seller would get suspended. This would happen only if a seller had done something very wrong.

I knew immediately that something was amiss. After investigating the details of the three suspensions, I learned that the products in question had all come from this "XYZ" company.

I reached out to Parker right away, and, in no uncertain terms, told him to refund all parties immediately.

"XYZ" issued refunds and I assumed this matter was closed and that this company would cease operations.

However, a short time later at an event that I held in Las Vegas for about 100 guests, a member of my program began telling me that he was out $10,000 because of an unscrupulous supplier. With a sinking feeling, I stopped him mid-sentence and asked whether the company involved was this "XYZ" company.

He answered, "Yes."

That night, I sent the owners of "XYZ" a few messages explaining that they must stop selling product; they must refund the member from whom they'd taken $10,000, and that if they comply with these remedies immediately, I would refrain from posting a public video regarding their misdeeds. I'm not in the habit of issuing warnings that I don't intend to see through, so, while awaiting a response, I had my videographer film me discussing the issues concerning "XYZ" and I had the video ready to post to my YouTube channel.

The next day, however, my member guest in Las Vegas reported that "XYZ" had, in fact, refunded his money.

"XYZ" then removed their online company information.

This series of events occurred in December 2018.

Some months passed and I did not hear anything further on the matter.

That was, until August 2019, when I began to hear that similar activity was occurring again.

This time around, I discovered that Parker's brother had set up a new company under a different name.

But—they were pulling the same deceptive sales stunts again.

My response to this distressing news was to make announcements about the issue during my online programs, as well as, warn the Facebook group members to stay away from this bogus business.

As disappointing as these circumstances were, in general, you do not have to worry that suppliers will try to scam you.

I will give you a tip that you can use which should help to keep you from getting involved with potentially unscrupulous suppliers: Simply do a quick search online for a "domain age lookup". Look at the age of the domain name of the supplier in question. If the domain has existed for only a few months, simply do not work with them. Wait a year and check back to see whether they are in business still. This should give you a better sense of their viability.

A MAP Disaster

In the retail industry there is a term called MAP (Minimum Advertised Price). In practical terms it means that no retailer, no Amazon seller, no online retailer, can sell a product at a price lower than the MAP.

In essence, this is a great component in retail because it means a seller won't need to worry about prices adjusting below a certain point, which then means sellers can expect a certain level of profit.

However, in reality, Amazon does not act as a supervisory agent for MAP.

MAP is an agreement between manufacturers, distributors, and retailers. Amazon is not a participant in this arrangement and therefore, it is up to the manufacturers, distributors and retailers to monitor and enforce the MAP.

My first encounter with MAP related issues happened while I was in high school, when I purchased some high-tech coffee makers. The MAP for this product was $219.99.

However, two weeks into selling these coffee makers, the price dropped below the MAP of $219.99.

At this point, more sellers entered the listing, and the MAP continued to drop lower and lower.

I had invested $45,000 into these coffee makers, and I ended up barely breaking even on this deal.

From this experience, I learned that if you're going to invest in a MAP deal, you should only consider investing when you are going to be one of only a few sellers allowed to sell the product. Specifically, this means that you need to have a written contract that all sellers agree to sign, that clearly defines the terms of the MAP.

When something is important enough, you do it even if the odds are not in your favor.

— Elon Musk

Chapter 14

Success Stories

The Amazon Army

The students' success stories that are featured in this book represent some of the superstar students out of the more than 4,000 people that have enrolled in my Online Retail Mastery course. While I can promise that my team and I will do our best to provide you with the knowledge and support you need to succeed with your Amazon business—I cannot guarantee your personal success. Every student is different, and each person will put forth a different level of effort and will take different degrees of action. I will give you the information and instruction that you need to be successful, but whether you succeed is, ultimately, up to you.

The case studies shared here are those of exceptional students who took substantial action in their Amazon businesses—and their results are not intended to be viewed as typical or average. Be sure to read our earnings disclaimer, which can be found at the beginning of this book and on the beaucrabill.com website. You need to be smart with the money you invest, calculate your own risks, and make sure you follow all the rules and proper procedure. You can strive to predict your sales, but there are no guaranteed outcomes.

I have not paid any of these students for their testimonials. Their original, video-taped testimonials can be found on my YouTube channel at: https://is.gd/beau_crabill_youtube.

The following transcripts of those video recordings have been edited slightly for purposes of conciseness and clarity but, as much as possible, the stories have been relayed in each student's own words.

Case Study 1: Joe and Hayden

Hayden: My name is Hayden Hogan, and I'm from Mobile, Alabama. Before enrolling in the Online Retail Mastery course, I was working as a sales rep for TruGreen.

My Dad owns a bunch of Planet Fitness franchises, and I've always known that I wanted to follow in his footsteps, to be an entrepreneur, but I never knew how to make that happen. When I was a naive 18-year-old with a credit card, I racked up a ton of unnecessary debt.

Since accruing that debt, I've been stuck in the 9-to-5 rat race, trying to pay it off.

Unfortunately, while working to pay off that debt, I got laid off.

Joe and I have been friends for five years. I've always known that he had a strong business mind and liked to think outside of the box, which is a trait I appreciate. We had always talked about starting some kind of venture together.

When I lost my job, I contacted him and said that we needed to figure something out.

We needed to figure out how to start a legitimate online business.

One night, I was up late scrolling social media—when an ad appeared on my phone. It was Beau, explaining his business model. I had never considered his type of strategy before, but it immediately made sense. A light bulb went off for me!

The next morning, I pitched the strategy to Joe. He thought it was genius. Beau's approach is based on a well-established retail strategy: Buy low, sell high. The approach has always worked in business, and always will.

We spent the day watching all of Beau's YouTube videos—and soon after, we were enrolled in Beau's course and then began taking action.

Joe: I'm Joe, and I've been buying and selling stuff my whole life. I'm from Sarasota, and after meeting Hayden—I always knew we'd get into business together, somehow.

When Hayden showed me Beau's videos, I couldn't believe it. All the other videos I had watched insisted on getting involved in private labeling and advertising, but I knew that those approaches were difficult and risky.

We knew we had to buy Beau's course.

We quickly found our first product, and it started selling almost immediately. We were amazed. The strategy works! From there, we just kept moving forward—moving and grooving.

Hayden: In the four years prior to finding Beau, I had considered getting involved in selling on Amazon. But everyone I spoke with or every message I encountered said that you had to do private labeling—such as, buying 10,000 generic phone chargers and hoping they'd sell. It seemed risky to me.

Joe: **Joe:** As soon as we bought Beau's course, we took action by getting our business license and getting our business set up and organized. We watched the course a couple of times all the way through, to make sure that we knew all of the information really well—and then before too long, we were selling!

Hayden: It took about a month to find our suppliers and then two additional weeks to get our first sales. Obviously, that first product was just a test—but that product led us to more products and suppliers. Soon after that, we went to the ASD trade show.

We had some minor hiccups, but as long as you take action, you'll be fine. We tried to get ungated to sell Microsoft products off the bat, but that didn't work.

Instead of getting frustrated, we just got started by selling something that didn't require ungating. Soon after, we were able to get ungated in Microsoft. We just asked our supplier for an invoice, and within 24 hours, Amazon had called, and then we were approved! Once we got ungated in Microsoft, that led to getting ungated with Sony, and then Nintendo, as well as a few others.

Joe: Our biggest struggle so far has just been keeping inventory in stock.

Hayden: Our products sell quickly. Our capital is decent and growing. Our lowest ROI has been 13 percent but it's a very quick mover. Our highest ROI was 29 percent.

We've figured out all of the logistics. We've built such good relationships with our suppliers that they give us too many good deals on products. We don't have enough money yet to invest in them all.

It's a good problem to have, but we need to keep building our capital in order to take advantage of everything we're offered. Off the top of my head, there are six products we want at this time but can't afford yet.

We started the course on February 21st, 2018. I'm writing this testimonial in June 2018.

Our main product categories are video games, sports and outdoors, and electronics.

Our best sales numbers over a 30-day period were $103,000. We actually ran out of stock in that deal, but, if we hadn't, we would have sold around $160,000.

With our lead times and reserves catching up, we should hit $250,000 or even $300,000 within the next couple of months.

Next year, our goal is to hit at least $5 million in sales. We're absolutely on track for that.

We don't need to make any changes. No retail stores to deal with, no warehouse—everything is done online. All we need is more capital, and that's on its way.

We've learned that there are probably 20 to 25 optimal product categories that you can focus on, and then after just finding a few good suppliers, you can concentrate on completely maxing out and dominating those categories.

Hiring a virtual assistant to keep things in stock might be helpful—but honestly, we enjoy the day-to-day logistics. It's fun. It's simple and fulfilling work. We won't need any help for at least a couple of years still, and we'll only need to hire help if we decide to go crazy scaling our business up into the millions of dollars in sales each year.

During the years I was supposed to be in college, I did door-to-door car sales. I was always working, so I could never take time off to visit my family. Now, I can work from anywhere with just my laptop. As I write this, I've been home visiting with my family for two weeks. I don't know when I'm leaving, because I can stay (and work right here) for as long as I want.

Joe: I just came back from a vacation with my family. Despite the fact that Hayden and I both travel around now, our business has continued running as smoothly as usual.

We're both truly grateful and we both enjoy this business.

A bunch of fellow students have contacted us, asking us questions regarding how they can find more suppliers and better products—when, they're already getting sales.

Beau preaches this lesson all the time—maybe they'll listen if they hear it from us too: Focus on relationships!

I can't stress this advice enough. Call your suppliers. Joke with them. Meet them. Send them letters. In one of his videos, Beau talks about buying his supplier's son a toy.

Take all this advice to heart. This is how you get the best deals. (And it's fun!)

When they (your supplier) has been working on a brand deal for a year and they finally get that deal—who do you think they're going to call first? Obviously, they'll call the person who has been the nicest to them, and the client who they know will pull the trigger immediately on a good deal.

We've been working with the same two or three suppliers for the last four months. We're friends with them now. We send them gifts. It pays off—we now have so many product opportunities that we can't possibly buy them all.

When you work with just two suppliers, you get to know them well. I have their personal phone numbers; visit their Facebook pages, and I follow their Instagram accounts. Get personal with them! You'll come to recognize that they're people who are just looking to do good business and who want to make money. Just like you and me.

Joe: Along the lines of building supplier relationships—while negotiating in your own favor is important, don't try to wrangle your supplier on your very first deal. Usually, it's worth it for you to concede a few extra bucks so that the supplier will favor you more in the long run. Most people choose to argue with them over pennies. If you are friendly with them and you just let them keep those few extra bucks, that will help build a long-lasting relationship.

Once you get this business going, you'll be able to do more and more of whatever you'd like to be doing in life. In the future, we are looking forward to having financial freedom, and to traveling the world, and spending more time with family—while still making a lot of money.

And we've already started to do just that, thanks to Beau.

Case Study 2: Tara

My name is Tara, and I'm from Iowa. I've been hustling and flipping products starting back when I was a teenager in high school. I remember going to school with $3 for lunch—and coming home with $25. My parents would give me $3 on Monday, and by Thursday I'd tell them to keep their money.

"I'm good. I've got $50," I'd tell them.

When I got a little older, I started flipping things on eBay.

I've always had that "Goonies" mentality—a treasure hunter who wants to win. After I got married, my husband and I flipped these buses with hydraulic handicap lifts. We'd buy them for $300 and sell them for $2,000.

That's always been my mindset. If I have a buck, I want to turn it into ten.

Three years ago, we bought an audio/video business and it has exploded—but so did our stress levels. We design and install sound systems for churches and performing arts centers. The money is good, but we constantly have to worry about maintenance and customer service. We've been looking for ways to remove ourselves from that business.

A few of my friends kept telling me about Amazon.

Now, we're getting close to transitioning to Amazon full-time—where we won't have to worry about dealing with the stress that comes with the audio/video business.

We started selling on Amazon a year and a half ago. I started by doing arbitrage—buying video games on Best Buy's website for $10 and selling them on Amazon for $50. My first month, I did a couple thousand bucks in sales. It was simple, but I couldn't see a way to scale it to a full-time income.

It was easy to maintain but difficult to grow.

About eight months into my Amazon business, I got my tonsils out and while I was recovering, I browsed YouTube for videos about selling on Amazon. I remember lying in bed, seeing Beau's stuff and thinking... who is this kid? Does he actually make a full-time income on Amazon?

I started tweeting him and asking questions. I'm sure some of my questions probably seemed dumb to him, but Beau always responded and helped me out. At some point, I realized that if I didn't invest in my business, it wasn't going to go anywhere.

So, I bought Beau's course. I got a lot out of the YouTube videos, but I wanted to expedite my learning process so that I could start making money. It was much smarter to opt to have Beau do all the groundwork for me.

Once I bought the course, I couldn't believe how easy it was. Everything was laid out, step-by-step, in videos.

But, I'll admit, I was afraid at first. I was used to buying, for example, 20 video games and not worrying too much whether they sold. Now I'd be working with suppliers, where I'd be considering buying 200 of those same video games (and felt like I'd be worrying like crazy whether they'd sell). It felt risky in the beginning, even though I knew the system was designed to eliminate risk.

I hesitated for a while, but at some point, I had to accept that I wouldn't be able to predict everything with perfect accuracy. I knew that I might make some mistakes, but overall—I felt that I would make out with a profit. If I bought something and it didn't sell, I'd be able to liquidate it somewhere else.

I accepted the bit of uncertainty, and I started taking action. Deciding to start was a struggle for me—I thought of myself as a winner, only picking guaranteed winning products—but I got over my anxiety.

I realized my win-loss ratio was still positive. I lost occasionally (say if a bunch of other people bought something at the same time as me and undercut me), but I won way more than I lost. If I "lost," I just liquidated the product and moved on to the next one.

When I bought the course, I was making $3,000 a month in sales. I immediately jumped up to $5,000 but scaling to $10,000 was a struggle with my own fears.

Once I cleared $10,000, however, that fear was erased—and I quickly grew to $20,000 a month and moved onwards! Really it was only my lack of confidence that had held me back.

Now, my only problem is keeping things in stock because they fly off the (digital) shelves. My most recent best seller is face serum. I just bought 200 units—and within a week, it was time to reorder again.

Besides that, my only issue is getting off track with multitasking. I'll say I want to find a video game supplier—but instead of focusing on finding and vetting one, I'll find six and get overwhelmed looking at all of their spreadsheets together. Fortunately, I came across Beau's "Time Management" module in his mastermind group, and things have started to get easier now in this area.

I've always believed that multitasking is the way to get stuff done, but now I realize that I need to take things one at a time.

I used to stare at a list of 1,000 products from a supplier and get upset if I felt that there was nothing to sell. It felt like a "loss." But I'm finally starting to accept that the smart thing, is to move on immediately—and realize that not every supplier will have something you need. That's the nature of the business. Move on and find another supplier.

Beyond that, the business has been pretty simple. I've had virtually no trouble getting ungated for any products. I just follow Amazon's instructions and Beau's guidelines provided in his course. Whenever I see that I'm restricted, I don't worry about it. I just go ahead, order the product and then get ungated.

I initially thought I'd sell products that I like. But then I stumbled upon good suppliers who happened to focus on products I didn't really have any interest in—health products, vitamins, face cream, hair products. Toy distributors. I realized that all of these products were profitable, so I tried to let go of my personal preferences and the things that were familiar to me. Now, I sell whatever can make me money.

If you get hung up on the idea of selling only one type of product, you'll overlook other good opportunities.

I never would have thought of looking for health care products, but they found me. If I had obsessed over finding a certain category of supplier, I may never have grown my business the way that I have.

In 12 months, I want to be doing this full-time. That's my goal.

I want to be more organized. I want to streamline my process so that I'm only ordering once a month. I've also been doing most of the shipping myself—so I need to study the parts of the course where Beau explains how to get suppliers to do the shipping.

I haven't worried about optimizing my business yet, but I know all the course content that I need is available. I just need to focus on learning and then get moving. There's no reason why I can't hit my goal of having a full-time business within a year, while making my income without stress.

I've realized that while growing the business takes a bit of time, maintaining it is extremely easy. Once my suppliers are set, I just need to maintain a relationship with them, and reorder products. I could easily do that in a couple hours a day.

Right now, I'm managing my Amazon business and our audio/visual business at the same time, without much trouble. I could definitely maintain producing $20,000 in sales a month on just a few hours a week. The more experience I get doing the online sales, the less time I need to get everything done. Growing takes a bit of time at first, but once you figure out the products—it becomes more like easy maintenance.

I've even used the course to start shipping my eBay sales via Amazon. I had no idea that doing so would save me money. That's been a game-changer, making me money and saving me time.

Also, almost everything I have listed on Amazon, I list on eBay, too. Worst-case scenario, I get at least a few extra sales. Why not?

These are advanced strategies I never could have found on regular YouTube videos—which is why I really appreciate the Online Retail Mastery course.

If you've been dragging your feet but you're now thinking about investing in yourself, just go for it. There's a money-back guarantee. What do you have to lose?

You can try to put all the puzzle pieces together yourself, but it will take much longer to figure things out on your own. How much is your time worth? Stop wasting time. Invest in your future and make it happen.

The stress of my Amazon business is nothing compared to my audio/video business. The peace of mind is priceless. There's no price you can put on peace of mind. I love the freedom. I love that I'm writing this from North Carolina, because I wanted to go to a concert, and was able to be away from home, while still operating my business. I love that while I was at the concert, I checked my phone and saw that I had sold $1,000 that day!

Making money while you're on vacation feels pretty amazing

Case Study 3: Joe

*Note from Beau Joe was one of my first students. He went through each section carefully, step-by-step, which is exactly what I recommend to each student. Joe is focused on higher-margin products.

I joined Beau in October 2017. I had tried private labeling and retail arbitrage enterprises, but those businesses were moving slowly. They're extremely hard to scale, and I knew neither could become a full-time business for me.

Online retail is so much easier to scale. You're buying products that are already selling. It's an easy formula, and it just comes down to how much time and money you can invest.

Now that I've been doing this for a few months, I'm working with a total of four suppliers. But I order consistently from just two of those suppliers. I've ordered fewer than 10 products, but I'm currently doing $1,200 a week.

My only regret is that I wish I started off by focusing on higher-ticket items. My first product had a decent ROI but sold at around ten to fourteen dollars. If I had waited to find a product around $50 (my highest-priced item, currently), I may have been able to scale quicker.

I've been selling toys—Barbie dolls, Fisher Price, and so forth. I've had no trouble getting ungated. The longest time it took me to get ungated with a product was about 24 hours.

The hardest part of this business is getting started. When you first speak with a supplier, you're both uncertain about each other. You don't know whether they'll have the right products and business operation that you are looking for—and they don't know whether you're a reliable person to work with.

Also, every supplier does things a little bit differently. At the beginning, I had to learn each of their systems. I kept emailing them messages asking, "What do I need to do next?" Once you get the system down, however, everything gets much easier.

My goal for the next year is to consistently hit $2,000 in sales per day. I can absolutely achieve that.

When you invest time and money into this business, the business scales itself. It's that simple. It can scale as big as you're willing to envision… and able to invest in.

Early on, I needed to invest time to learn the system. The course is a lot of information to take in. I spent three to four hours per day during the first couple of weeks—and then I focused on practicing and applying.

Now, the system works basically by itself. I spend around thirty minutes a day on my Amazon business—an hour at most. Mostly, it's just accounting and maintenance, making sure I'm tracking everything and adjusting the Buy Box price if needed.

At first, I sold whatever products would make me money.

My first order was 200 units—and I was able to reorder 500 units soon thereafter. But then I focused on one-off deals on toys for the holidays. My ROI has ranged from 20 percent to 80 percent. Toys have had the best ROI for me.

Now, I'm looking for more utility type products—stuff like kitchenware and office supplies that people need and order consistently, rather than things that are more nonessential goods. I'm focusing on products that I can consistently reorder to virtually guarantee profits.

A big thanks to Beau for all the sacrifices he makes for his students. I appreciate all the knowledge he has provided.

Without Beau, I don't know whether I'd have an online business at all.

Now, I feel free.

Case Study 4: Monica

*Monica, who's in her mid-twenties, had never sold on Amazon before taking my course. Now, she's doing over $8,000 a month in sales.

I joined Beau about five months ago, while working five to six days a week at a restaurant. I had to schedule my Amazon hours around my work hours, so it wasn't easy in the beginning. I was always exhausted.

But I needed my day job in order to build up my capital.

My first challenge was to find good suppliers. I had a massive list to sort through, but had to go through a ton of their spreadsheets before finding one that I wanted to invest in. Once that happened though, I wanted to place an order right away.

In the beginning, I focused on finding any supplier that had a product with a decent ROI. Now that I'm more established, I'm focusing on the beauty category. I had to get approved in the beauty and topical categories, but, I used one of the ungating companies that Beau had recommended in the Online Retail Mastery course, and got approved in a week.

Most people can get ungated in a day, but I was just starting out. Getting ungated in a week was pretty good, considering that I had zero sales on my Amazon account.

My first few products sold quickly, and I made almost $9,000 in sales—but then I sold out. I wish I had ordered more inventory, but not buying enough is better than buying too much.

Now, I know exactly what to do next time.

My goal is to scale this as quickly as possible and grow my business as large as possible too. As soon as it's reasonable to do, I want to quit my job so that I can have more free time.

I have confidence that I can scale this up to a big business, because this business is all about numbers. As long as I run the numbers and know that my ROI is sufficient—and then I double-check to make sure those numbers are accurate, and account for some fluctuation—I have virtually nothing to lose.

You can't go wrong.

One of the best parts of this has been the student Facebook group. I've been amazed at how supportive everyone has been—helping each other grow their businesses. It's an invaluable asset to have.

Even though Amazon has done most of the work for me—handling everything else once I've found the products—this is absolutely a **real** business. Amazon is a multi-billion-dollar company. There are people that make millions selling on Amazon.

Trust in the system and keep moving forward. Since Beau knows the business so well, his advice can be really succinct. You might have to read through a lesson a few times over or watch a video more than once to truly understand all the instructions. But if you're patient and keep taking action, you'll do well.

Before you know it, you'll understand online retail inside and out.

Beau is so awesome and supportive. I was completely brand new to this—and now I have a real business. Without him, I would have had no pathway out of my stressful job. Now, I do.

Case Study 5: Shane

*Note from Beau: Shane is a firefighter from Michigan with a wife and kids. He's an awesome, humble guy. After seeing my ads on YouTube, he was wondering whether my Action-Based Guarantee was legitimate, so he asked me how many people I'd refunded.

I explained that I've refunded every single person who has asked for a refund, according to the terms in the guarantee. However, that has only been a handful of people—and most of them didn't provide any real reason for why they wanted a refund. They just marked 'miscellaneous details' on the refund form. Regardless, I gave them their money back. The course just wasn't for them.

After sending this reply to Shane, I didn't hear back from him for another month. Then, he sent me this message:

"I don't know if you remember me, but I bought the course and just did $20,000 in sales this month in my Amazon store."

This is Shane's story:

Before I started selling on Amazon, I sold various things on eBay. I was doing alright, but there was no way I could scale my eBay business. I only sold things when people in my network had items to give me, and I didn't have time to list everything and wait for sales.

I started searching around the Internet and noticed that other people were selling on Amazon, so, I thought, why shouldn't I give it a try? Soon after, I found Beau's Facebook page… and the rest is history.

Once I bought the course, I laid low and took time to learn the material. I'm not the type of guy who just jumps into things headfirst.

As I watched the videos, I took notes and printed off all of the forms that Beau has created. By doing that upfront, I save a lot of time now. People get stuck in the coursework and feel the need to ask a million questions as they go—but the answers are almost always in the course material already.

I just check my notes and nine times out of ten, the answer is right in front of me, plain and simple.

Also, Beau frequently adds new material—so make sure you keep your notes organized so that you can adjust them over time. Make them easy to find and easy to change. Mine are all saved in a Word document and numbered according to the course organization.

I document and track everything, so I can tell you exactly how long it took to get my business going.

On January 14th, I bought the course. On January 29th, I made my first small purchase to test the waters.

Looking back, I got pretty lucky. I rushed the order a bit, but I also sold out quicker than expected. I guess I had gotten a little antsy to get started, after reading everyone's Facebook posts about how well they were doing.

Once I completed the first order and everything had sold, I waited another two weeks to make a second purchase. I didn't want to rush again—in case the success of the first order had just been good luck.

When you're just starting out, don't compare yourself to other people. There's no rush to make your first purchase. Do it once you're ready.

In the past 30 days, I've sold about $15,000—but things are about to take off even more than that. I just attended the ASD Trade Show (as well as Beau's mastermind course in Las Vegas), and I bought a bunch of really profitable products at the ASD Trade Show. I also made connections that will pay off, big time.

I considered investing more before the show, but Beau advised me to wait. I could be selling a lot more today, but I will more than make up for holding off, with the purchases and with the connections I ended up making at ASD. It was great advice for the long run.

Basically, I'm short on products and inventory, and I still did $15,000 in sales last month. Next month, I should be able to do way more.

Everything has gone well since I started. I've only had trouble getting ungated once—I was trying to sell Crayola products and my invoice didn't work. But I listened to Beau's advice and I didn't panic. I contacted Amazon and asked them to look at my case again. I had used the distributor before, without any problems so I assumed that getting turned down by Amazon had to be a mistake. I submitted the same invoice again.

The next day, I was approved! If you follow the proper procedure for getting ungated, you shouldn't have any problems.

I've found a ton of suppliers, but I only work with three in total. I spend most of my money with two of those suppliers. The third one mainly works with brick and mortar stores and sells his excess stuff to me.

Those two distributors supply me with more products than I could possibly afford at this time. Right now, I'm out of investment cash—I'm just waiting for the rest of my inventory to be put in stock and to start selling.

Trust Beau's advice when he says to invest in building good business relationships with a small number of suppliers, before branching out too much.

I remember emailing Beau early on, freaking out because my suppliers only had small items.

Beau told me, "Calm down. Just order all of his small products to get his attention."

That's what I did. I placed a $15,000 order, and, suddenly, the supplier loved me. He started getting me deals. That supplier is one of my two main suppliers, now.

I was connected with a good supplier already; I just couldn't see it. Once I realized I had to earn the good deals from this supplier, everything changed for the better.

You can't really tell if a supplier is going to pay off until you place a couple of orders and then wait to see how they respond. This supplier was immediately appreciative and helpful.

Now that my business is on cruise control, I'm just waiting for my products to sell and considering my next way of branching out. I actually just enrolled in Beau's eBay course—and even though I've been selling on eBay since 2005, I've already learned a bunch of new and useful things.

I never knew how to optimize a description for mobile.

I've always said: You're never too old or too experienced to learn something new.

Beau is twenty years younger than I am. I don't care about that. I learn from him all the time. I guarantee I could go to anybody on this planet and find something they could teach me that I didn't know, regardless of their age.

When I emailed Beau about his refund policy, I thought his course was too good to be true.

After I got his response, I realized I could trust Beau's character. I have seen that there are some negative comments about the course on Facebook. Most are positive, but, of course, there is some negative feedback. Beau always lets everyone know that if they're not happy with the program, just let him know and he will issue a refund.

If you're not happy with what Beau is providing, he doesn't take it personally.

I've had fourteen people contact me privately from Beau's page. They always ask if I'm legitimate and if he's legitimate. I've replied so many times to this question already that I started to co-py-paste my responses, because I always say the same thing:

> "I'm a real person. Check my Facebook page. I have a family. If I wasn't making money with Beau's system, I sure as heck wouldn't be talking about it."

I talk about this program because some people need a kick in the butt to buy the course. It's going to help you. I paid for the course, and yet I still feel like I owe Beau money. I've only been learning for about three months, and I've already made well past the amount I invested.

I would recommend Beau and his course to anybody.

My final piece of advice is: Be patient. Whatever information you are looking for is likely somewhere in the course. I've watched it over and over again, and I always find the answers I need.

Beyond that, as I said, don't compare yourself to others in the group. Don't compare yourself to Beau. Just go at your own pace and get started when you're ready.

Some people have trouble finding distributors, but to me that part was extremely easy. There are tons of methods in the course that show you how to do this. I had so many, my only problem was weeding them out to find the best ones. Now, I've done that as well.

At one point, I was hoping to find one more distributor, so I just asked one of my current ones if he would recommend any. He immediately gave me the name of his distributor, and suddenly, I had another good supplier to work with.

Because I've built relationships, my distributors help me. The last thing I bought came about because of a phone call I got from one of my suppliers. He knew I was ungated to sell beauty products, and that's why he contacted me. I ran the numbers and immediately made the purchase.

I got the offer before anyone else even saw it. No email blast to the masses. It was an easy purchase.

It took a couple of months to get to that point, but now I'm set.

Before buying the course, I had developed a business model and projected I would make around $173,000 a year in profits. But that was before I understood the full potential of this business. Last time I checked; I was 17 percent ahead of my projections. Without digging into the numbers, I can say with confidence that I could be making around $500,000 in profits within five years.

I'm committed to this long term, and I pour every single bit of money that I can, back into my business.

Recently, people around me have asked how I'm accomplishing all that I am achieving.

Obviously, I forward them Beau's website and the course name, and I give a glowing recommendation.

Some people look into the program for themselves, but others have wanted to give me money to invest in the business, so that they can just take a cut of the action. I'm considering that now, but after just a few months in this business—I don't yet consider myself ready to take that on.

Down the road, I may let people invest in my business activity. For now, I'm just focused on learning as much as possible, and on growing.

Finally, before investing in Beau's program, I tried to do this business on my own for three months and I got nowhere. As simple as it is to be an online seller once you've gone through Beau's course, there are just too many layers in this business, to go into it blind and try to figure out what to do all by yourself.

I owe all my success to Beau and his Online Retail course.

Additional student testimonials can be found on YouTube at: https://is.gd/student_testimonials.

Life is growth. Your grow or you die.

— Phil Knight

Chapter 15

The Future of My Amazon Business

My Amazon business has taken me on a journey such that I could never have imaged, as a young man growing up in a rural part of Washington State.

There is an expression; "It's not what you get when you achieve your goals in life—it's who you become in the process, that matters most." I have grown up while pursuing my wildest entrepreneurial dreams—as an online reseller—and have realized success well beyond anything I imagined when I first started out on this path.

As you read in an earlier chapter, this venture started with the adolescent idea of selling socks on eBay from my family home in Olympia. Eventually, those simple sock sales evolved into an incredibly successful business of selling brand name products on Amazon. Even upon reaching the high point of increasing my Amazon sales to over $100,000 per month, I realized there were still higher peaks to scale and new avenues to discover.

After living my entire life in the state of Washington, I decided that I wanted to explore other places. My business success had opened up an incredible world of possibilities for me. For my first stop, I chose a 300 square foot apartment just steps from Santa Monica's beaches in sunny Southern California. I spent my time running my business as well as literally running along the beautiful California shoreline each day. I was an independent adult, out on my own and making my way in the world.

Around this time, my dad introduced to me the person who would eventually become my business mentor and close friend. This person has advised me on business related matters and has provided counsel on other aspects of life as well. That person is Steven Sitkowski.

While I was in Santa Monica, Steven suggested that my next move should be to relocate to his home base in Utah, so that we could work together more readily while developing webinars and marketing concepts for my educational business. With this new plan and Steven's excellent coaching, my online course sales rose to nearly a quarter of a million dollars per month. This was a thrilling pinnacle, especially because I had not yet turned 21 years old. Imagine running a small empire while not yet being old enough to buy a beer. Pretty amazing. On a personal note, the fact is that I don't have any interest in beer, or in drinking any kind of alcohol, for that matter. Personally, I have watched liquor destroy people's lives and I cannot help but be influenced by those experiences and observations. I just think I'm better off without it. I have set some incredible and challenging goals for myself—goals that will take a lot of commitment and focus—and I wouldn't want to risk having something so superfluous as drinking interfere with those awesome plans.

So, where does a 21-year-old go from here, you may wonder? I can tell you this, my story and my business successes have only just begun!

Regarding the future of my business; The next phase is two-pronged.

First, I plan to be the preeminent provider of Amazon education, coaching and tools for students entering and navigating this dynamic online sales industry. I want to help make the journey into e-commerce seamless for hundreds of thousands of students all over the world. I will accomplish this objective by introducing would-be Amazon sellers to my sales expertise, my strategies and business planning through my YouTube videos, Instagram and Facebook pages, as well as, through my webinars, public speaking engagements, and joint ventures with other educational companies. I will stay on the cutting edge of the online retailing world and will always have the most advanced strategies available in the marketplace, because I will continue to work the business daily, myself. I'm excited to think of the countless number of people who will find business successes of their own—because of the education and guidance they find in this book alone.

The second facet of my future plan is; I am creating a fund named, The Crabill New Economy Fund. My mentor, Mr. Sitkowski, comes from the world of investing, where he has had decades of experience investing in the stock market. Initially, when I revealed to Steven how I was able to generate 10 to 20 percent profits on my inventory, and that I was able to turn over that inventory within a month or so, he suggested that we meet with one of his long-time investment associates in order to discuss setting up a fund specifically for buying merchandise to be sold on Amazon. As I've explained in this book, the beautiful thing about doing business with Amazon is that it's a scalable enterprise. Amazon logged sales of $141 billion in 2018, up 20% from the previous year. I envision a fund with $100 million in capital, which will eventually provide investors with returns not attainable in the stock market (and returns that, in my opinion, carry comparatively less risk). Currently, the fund is being beta tested using our own capital and it has been enjoying very predictable and highly profitable returns to date. I'm eager for the day when I will be able to offer this fund to the investing public, including, to those students of mine who are looking for passive income opportunities.

In addition to the comprehensive educational platform and the Crabill New Economy Fund, future plans also include acquiring suppliers, both to benefit my own business, as well as, to provide a way to make it easier for my students to find quality products at wholesale prices. Assuming the highest and best results come to fruition, there is the possibility that I could then choose to invest in my own Amazon warehouses. There is simply no ceiling for the person who does not cease reaching for the stars.

The best way for you to keep up with all the changes and all the growth happening with my company and with all the progress going on with the fund, is through our website: crabillcapital.com. Make sure to check out the latest news and information posted to my social media outlets and make time to catch my webinars online. Links to those resources can be found at beaucrabill.com. These resources are full of vital information that will keep you up to date on all industry related trends and activity.

This chapter shared all the exciting details regarding the future vision for my Amazon business. Now, the question is… what will the future of YOUR Amazon business look like?

One purpose of this book is to help you envision the incredible opportunities that are available to you, by becoming an Amazon reseller. I've provided a step-by-step strategy to help you get started (and I've presented methods that can help make your existing business even more profitable). I hope that you will have both the confidence and initiative, to move forward and take action in your own business life. It is obvious that Amazon is going to become more and more dominant in the retail space. There is little risk of market saturation any time in the foreseeable future. My recommendation to you is to make the most of this prime opportunity.

I'll be here to guide you every step of the way.

The time is always right to do what is right.

— Martin Luther King Jr.

Conclusion

If you follow me on any of my social media channels you most likely have caught a YouTube Live, an Instagram story, a Facebook post, a tweet, or a linked article where I share some of my personal viewpoints. (If you are not following me yet, I suggest doing so now. You can find all my social media links at beaucrabill.com.)

Before you close this book (and before you post your review of it), there are some key points I'd like to address. First, you must give yourself a reasonable amount of time before you should expect to feel really confident about your ability to operate in this business. You CAN succeed. This business is not rocket science. (Thank goodness!) You just need to allow adequate time to learn, to ask questions, to practice and prepare, so that all goes well and as planned when you make that first order. To quote Alexandre Dumas: "Nothing succeeds like success."

Second, of all the strategies or instructions or insights or tips that I've put forth in this book, you need to keep one crucial component in mind: **Buy low and sell high.**

Yes, the bottom line to achieving success in this business revolves around the fundamental strategy of buying low and selling high.

And finally, how can you best apply all the lessons and tips that I have presented to you?

Read carefully.

Pay attention.

Start small.

The most disheartening thing you can do in this business is lose money on your first order. If you lose money on your first order, it is likely that you won't feel like pursuing this business further.

Right? Helping you to avoid failure has been a primary motivator for developing my course. As I've mentioned, I didn't have the luxury of having a real mentor when I got into this business, nor did I have any sort of manual to follow. My own trial and error during my ten years of selling online has taught me exactly what to do and what not to do. The training I provide to students is designed to reduce risk, maximize opportunity, and flatten the learning curve.

And last, I want to leave you with a few words concerning my personal beliefs regarding the biggest factors that will impact your chances for success in this business. At my live events I touch on the importance of good habits and the critical life lessons I have learned that will be applicable to your business life as well. The topics and lessons I've covered in this book and in my online courses provide all the industry-related knowledge you need to succeed in this business. The other critical part of the success equation comes down to your personal habits, your mindset, and your work ethic. I am a firm believer that our habits define us and define the lives we get to live—for better or for worse. In this book, I talked about the financial benefit of

compound interest. In addition, you must understand the impact of compounding habits. These two principles work in much the same way with regard to their effect on your quality of life. The patterns you repeat in your life, even the little things, eventually yield the kind of life you will live.

Thank you for reading my book.

Remember: **Buy low and sell high.**

Now, go get started!

Made in the USA
Lexington, KY
02 December 2019